# The Dog
# Ate My Homework

# The
# Dog
# Ate My Homework

*Personal Responsibility—*
*How We Avoid It and What to Do About It*

# Vincent Barry

ANDREWS AND McMEEL

A UNIVERSAL PRESS SYNDICATE COMPANY

KANSAS CITY

**Library of Congress Cataloging-in-Publication Data**

Barry, Vincent E.
    The dog ate my homework  :  personal responsiblity—how we avoid it and what to do about it/Vincent Barry.
        p.    cm.
    Includes bibliographical references.
    ISBN 0-8362-2715-8 (hd)
    1. Responsibility.    I. Title.
BJ1451.B36    1997
158'.1—dc20                                                    96-38331
First Printing, March 1997                                    CIP
Second Printing, September 1997

ATTENTION: SCHOOLS AND BUSINESSES

Andrews and McMeel books are available at quantity discounts with bulk purchase for educational, business, or sales promotional use.
For information, please write to:
Special Sales Department, Andrews and McMeel, 4520 Main Street, Kansas City, Missouri 64111.

To Jeannine

*Here's* another fine mess you've gotten me into!

# Acknowledgments

Writing, says novelist Iris Murdoch, is like getting married. "One should never commit oneself until one is amazed at one's luck." I have four women to thank for the amazing luck that kept me committed to this book without having to be committed.

—Gareth Esersky at Carol Mann Agency, who gives lie to Shakespeare's admonition: "Let every eye negotiate for itself / And trust no agent." Not trust Gareth? Why, I wouldn't even cut the cards.

—Chris Schillig, my editor at Andrews and McMeel, who succeeds in making business fun and fun her business.

—Ruthanne Girvin, who typed and retyped the manuscript without temper or plaint.

—And last but foremost, my wife, Jeannine, companion of the work at every turn, and at every turn its working companion.

Amazing luck!

# Contents

# The Dog
# Ate My Homework

# Part I

~~~~~~~~~~~~~~~~~~~~~~~

## Avoiding Personal Responsibility

# Introduction:
# Language of Excuse
# and Evasion

According to the Bible, God sought out Adam and Eve after they had eaten the forbidden fruit and asked them, "What is this thou hast done?" "The serpent tricked us," they replied. Earlier Adam had blamed Eve: "The woman made me do it."

In his popular *Book of Virtues*, William Bennett calls this " She made me/He made me do it" "an archetypal drama reenacted in every generation where siblings and playmates are called upon to account for their misdoings." But we don't always outgrow this sort of immaturity. Sometimes it extends right into adulthood. Indeed, as Bennett says, "Nearly everyone has an excuse when something goes wrong."[1]

It's fashionable today to decry the absence of personal responsibility in others, but rarely in ourselves. The ablebodied man who prefers the dole to honest work; the unmarried teen who has a baby, and the welfare mother who has still another; the drunk driver, the drug addict, the deadbeat dad—these are the irresponsible ones. It's individuals like these who aren't taking charge of themselves and their conduct, not owning and owning up to their actions. They're the immature ones—not you and certainly not me. Like selfishness, irresponsibility is that detestable vice we're quick to spot in others, but slow to see in ourselves.

It's been said that the easiest person to deceive is oneself. There is, perhaps, no matter in which we're more susceptible to self-deception than personal responsibility. The fear of blame and punishment, of being cast out of our personal Edens, can be so fierce that we're capable of not only disowning but rationalizing our misdeeds. For this purpose we routinely employ an array of familiar expressions that, taken collectively, constitute a sort of conventional language of excuse and evasion. Some examples:

- My health care and business ethics students (at a large community college in southern California) don't always plainly admit that they procrastinated when they miss an assignment deadline. They talk instead of not having enough time, or being "spread too thin." I'm no better. When I don't return their assignments promptly, I'm inclined to cast myself as a victim of the dreaded "things," as in "It's been one *thing* after another" or "*Things* just piled up on me" (rarely "I let things pile up").

- *Lost shipment, bad weather, busy schedule, family problems*— of all excuses building contractors give for not completing a job on time, do you ever hear, "It was my fault. I was unprepared and unorganized"?

- Who of us hasn't heard the politician attempt to paper over unvarnished stupidity, insensitivity, or boorishness with an insincere, "I was only kidding" or "I surely didn't mean any disrespect" or "That certainly wasn't my intent"? In institutional life, it seems, individuals rarely take the blame for anything. They were "out of the loop" or "mistakes were made."

- It's become commonplace for various professionals to rebuff criticism of their conduct with a breezy, "I'm just doing my job"—thus the trial attorney who will do anything to win, even bend the truth. Or the reporter who invades the most intimate of privacies and makes an antique of common decency. Apparently, "The public has a right to know" what goes on behind closed doors, even if it's none of the public's business.

- And then, of course, there's the cornucopia of psychobabble any of us can enlist to excuse a misspent, misguided, and messed-up life. "I didn't get all the love I needed." Never mind that few do and no one knows how much is enough. "I need to get in touch with my inner child." Meanwhile my outer adult is running amok. "I'm an adult child of an alcoholic parent." Is anyone the product of perfect parenting? As for the unlucky few who weren't raised by certifiable parents, well, they needn't worry. They can always fall back on their position in the brood as the youngest, middle, eldest, or only child. Or, perhaps, they were the designated "rescuer," "outlaw," or "scapegoat." If all else fails, there's always the doomsday defense: "I never asked to be born," "I guess that's just the way I am," or "I'm only human, you know."

So of all the talk these days about personal responsibility, what can be said? It's both warranted and misdirected, I believe. *Warranted* because so many of us so-called adults are pitifully immature; *misdirected* because in our immaturity we tend to blame others far more than ourselves. We aim at perhaps valid but easy targets—welfare moms, illegal immigrants, promiscuous teens, and similar petitioners who are "taking advantage of the system." It's they who are lacking in the stern virtue of responsibility and must be brought to heel—thus the much ballyhooed Personal Responsibility Act, chilling proof that "political language . . . is designed to give the appearance of solidity to pure wind."[2]

But if we're truly serious about personal responsibility, we must start with ourselves. We need to learn to blame others less and ourselves more. Basic to all learning, growth, and positive behavioral change is awareness. In order to become more responsible, then, we initially need to become aware of our own immaturity, conscious of the myriad ways we ourselves attempt to duck responsibility and unconsciously may be teaching our children to. How can we develop such awareness? For me there's no better first step than becoming aware of the language of evasion and excuse.

"Language," said Walt Whitman, "is not an abstract construction of the learned, or of dictionary-makers, but is something arising out of the work, needs, ties, joys, affections, tastes, of long generations of humanity, and has its bases broad and low, close to the ground."[3] If the immaturity of disowning our actions and their outcomes often continues into adulthood, rest assured we'll see evidence of it "close to the ground"—in our popular expressions and familiar sayings, in our empty rhetoric and vacuous colloquialisms, in our knee-jerk responses and shibboleths. There we'll discover the language of avoidance, which both reflects and reinforces our immaturity. There, too, we can join the battle against the bewitchment of our intelligence with respect to self-responsibility.

The language of excuse and evasion bewitches our intelligence because it trades on three common and often valid defenses against blame. The first and most obvious of these is the straightforward denial of having done something, or simply: *"I didn't do it."* What we didn't do, we can't rightly be blamed for doing. The second defense against blame is an admission of having done something, but *unknowingly,* as in: *"I didn't know it."* What we legitimately didn't have full knowledge of usually reduces blame. The third of the defenses is also an admission of having done something, but unwillingly—*"I couldn't help it."* Again, what we truly couldn't help doing we ordinarily aren't entirely to blame for.

It's precisely because "I didn't do it," "I didn't know it," and "I couldn't help it" *can be* legitimate defenses against blame that they're subject to the three categories of abuse that I call *shifting the blame, playing dumb,* and *stacking the deck.* These categories constitute the field on which the blame game is played. Within them we'll discover the language of disowning that we need to become aware of as a first step toward becoming more personally responsible.

## Shifting the Blame: *"The Dog Ate My Homework"*

"It is not how you win or lose," goes the saying, "it's how you place the blame." Happily, in my nearly thirty years in the education "game"—teaching a variety of subjects from composition and literature to logic and critical thinking to philosophy and ethics—I've never had a student actually blame a dog for eating her homework. But in a manner of speaking, I've had many tell stories of assignment-consuming canines, ranging from shaggy friends to mangy machines. A sampling:

"My girlfriend was supposed to turn it in."
"My father was on my case all night."
"The boss made me work late."
"Another paper was due today."
"It's locked in my boyfriend's car."
"The clock didn't go off this morning (which made me late and hurry and forget)."
"The computer wiped it out."

Doubt if you dare, but homework-eating hounds definitely dog some students.

Of course, blameworthy mutts aren't confined to schools or owned solely by students. They can be found any-where—at home, work, or play; in any activity or role; throughout all institutions at every level. Presto, we can make dogs appear at any time or place, under any circum-stance, whenever we wish to disown responsibilities for our actions by shifting the blame to someone or something else. But these "dogs" rarely are as obvious as the ones students are inclined to summon. They're more subtle, and thus more likely to escape our notice and win our acceptance. So we need to be careful. Without ever realizing it, we may be placing the fault in ourselves in our "dogs." We may be say-ing, "I didn't do it," when in fact we did.

## *Playing Dumb:*
## *"I Didn't Know the Gun Was Loaded"*

In handling guns, it's always best to assume they're loaded—even BB guns. That's common sense. Yet, every year hundreds of people are accidentally shot by individuals whose only excuse is "I didn't know the gun was loaded." About all their surviving victims can say is "You should have known."

Certainly there are times when ignorance is excusable. Some things we really couldn't know or reasonably be expected to know. Then "I didn't know" is a legitimate excuse that ordinarily reduces our responsibility and blame. Indeed, it's precisely because ignorance *can* be a good excuse that we're not shy about pleading it, even when it isn't.

The Bible records that when God confronted Cain after Abel's death, Cain denied his crime. "Where is Abel your brother?" God asked him. "I do not know," Cain replied. "Am I my brother's keeper?" (Genesis 4:9). Cain, of course, did know where Abel was. But he wanted to avoid blame and punishment. So he feigned ignorance. He played dumb.

Now, the gun shooter who truthfully says, "I didn't know the gun was loaded" is a moral cut above Cain. He is, after all, not lying and he didn't intend any harm. But he's not blameless. Whereas Cain denied what he knew, the gun shooter denies what he should have known: that guns can be loaded and, therefore, should be handled with care. So, although truthful, he's nonetheless culpably ignorant. He's more Cain-like than he might at first appear to be. For he, too, is not wanting to own up to his actions. Like Cain, he's playing dumb in order to avoid blame and punishment.

So was Beverly Russell, the stepfather of Susan Smith, the woman who received a thirty-five-year prison sentence for drowning her two young children. During Smith's sentence hearing, Russell said that he would have acted more responsibly toward his stepdaughter had he known she would end up killing her children. Apparently what the political and religious activist meant was that he wouldn't have sexually abused her as he had done for years. Nobody can say for sure what would have happened had Russell acted like a father rather than a sexual predator. But that he should have known better is indisputable. He should have known not only the evil of his conduct, but its dark, long-term potential. To that he was playing dumb, and for that he's responsible.

If Beverly Russell should have known better, so should we. We should know better than to run red lights, bike without helmets, smoke, overeat, underexercise, have unprotected sex, and bear children we can't provide for. We should know better than to cheat, deceive, and exploit others or violate their trust. We should also know better than to think that ours are the only rights that count, that our interests and needs always come first. Mature, responsible adults honor others as they themselves wish to be honored. They recognize and respect the bonds created by special relationships, and accept the blame for breaking them. This means, for example, that when individuals and families are wounded, sometimes irreparably, by extramarital affairs, grown-ups don't say, "If I had known the heartbreak it would cause, I never would have had this affair." That's as much a copout as Beverly Russell's saying, "If I'd only known . . ."

The point is that there's a variety of ways that, figuratively speaking, we claim "I didn't know the gun was loaded." Common to each is not squarely facing the facts, but playing dumb to them in order to do or get what we want and to avoid the blame for it.

## Stacking the Deck: "My Mother Was a Junkie, My Father Was a Drunk"

About midway through the musical *West Side Story*, members of a street gang satirically explain to a beat cop why they are the way they are:

> *Dear kindly Sergeant Krupke,*
> *You gotta understand*
> *It's just our bringin' upke*
> *That's got us out of hand.*
> *Our mothers all are junkies,*
> *Our fathers all are drunks.*
> *Golly Moses, natcherly we're punks!*[4]

The Jets, as the gang is called, go on to sing about how they're "very upset" because they never got all the love "ev'ry child oughta get." One member says that if he's a mess, it's because "my sister wears a mustache, my brother wears a dress." In brief, the street toughs are totally misunderstood. They're not bad, just "sociologically sick"— victims of some "terrible trick" played on them by society. So, naturally, they're punks.

Most of us probably are like the Jets now and again. Caught in a mistake or misdeed that won't allow a plausible "I didn't do it" (shifting the blame) or "I didn't know it" (playing dumb), we're apt to say, "I couldn't help it." Like the Jets, we attempt to avoid responsibility and blame by claiming we were powerless to do anything else but what we did.

Sometimes it's true: We couldn't have acted otherwise. Compelling circumstances ordinarily reduce responsibility. No one can reasonably be held accountable for what was impossible to do or avoid doing. So, genuine powerlessness, like reasonable ignorance, usually is blame-limiting.

But we can be mistaken about our relative freedom. We can think we have less power than we actually do. What we say or believe lies outside our control in fact may be well within it. What we insist we couldn't help doing, perhaps we really didn't have to do at all. And what we failed to do, because we believed we had no other choice, perhaps we could have done. In short, the powerlessness we feel or proclaim may not be real but illusory.

Although pseudo-powerlessness no more excuses than culpable ignorance does, that makes it no less popular an excuse-abuse. Shifting the blame and playing dumb may be our first lines of defense. But when neither is plausible, "stacking the deck" will do—making ourselves appear powerless and, therefore, blameless.

At play and in life, "stacking the deck" ensures by pre-arrangement a particular outcome—winning in a card game, innocence in the blame game. Like a deck of cards that can be prearranged so as to increase the chance of winning, a body of facts can be manipulated so as to make one look helpless and, therefore, innocent. That's what the Jets were doing. Thus, if they were "depraved," it was because they were "deprived." If they were antisocial, it was because they suffered from a "social disease" called delinquency. If they were delinquents, it was because they were the off-spring of delinquent parents, who "didn't wanna have me, but somehow I was had." In other words, they had no say in how they would live their lives. Conditions outside their power to influence made them the way they were and compelled them to act as they did.

Available to any of us is an array of figurative "mother-junkies" and "father-drunks" for disempowering ourselves, and thereby avoiding responsibility for our lives. Biology serves the purpose for those of us convinced that our lives would be substantially better "if only" we were another color or the other sex; "if only" we were taller, richer, thinner; "if only" our nose were shorter and our teeth straighter. Lots of us who aren't genetic hostages are circumstantial ones. Believing ourselves to be caught in webs of circumstance, we feel trapped, helpless, doomed. "What else can I do?" we ask, when perhaps we're actually unwilling to face what we should or need to do. "My hands are tied," we tell ourselves, when maybe it's not freedom we lack, but courage. "You gotta go along to get along," we chant, as if success through conformity were a natural law. And when that saw backfires, we alibi, "I was just doing what I was told to do," as if blind obedience confers absolution.

When all else fails—in the absence of any other credible, power-limiting excuse—we can always fall back on my personal favorite: those "things that just happen." Life's technical difficulties beyond our control. Thus, it's never I who make a perfect ass of myself, but that *something* that got into or came over me—that *thing,* whatever it is, that inhabits me when "I'm not myself today." That *thing* that can upend even the high and mighty, and compel them to act utterly out of character—like the prominent politician who responded vaguely to reports that he was having extramarital affairs while running a campaign espousing family values in 1978. "In the late 1970s," this most powerful man allowed, "things happened—period."[5] Alas, more putty in the hands of the dreaded *things*.

The chorus of the Jets, then, is wide and deep. "Gee, Officer Krupke" has many versions. Some are obvious, most less so. All involve not acknowledging real options and genuine freedom but stacking the deck to give the appearance of blame-mitigating circumstances.

There are numerous familiar expressions and popular sayings that often function, both logically and psychologically, as the equivalencies of "The dog ate my homework," "I didn't know the gun was loaded," or "My mother was a junkie, my father was a drunk." Part One of this brief book presents seventeen of them. Although some fall rather neatly into one or the other of the three categories of avoidance— shifting the blame, playing dumb, and stacking the deck— others are open to multiple interpretations. In the end, the precise labeling of the expression matters little. Vastly more important is recognizing it for what it often is: a rhetorical dodge for disowning our actions and their outcomes. With awareness of the various ways we may be avoiding responsibility, we can then turn to the practical question of what to do about it, which is addressed in Part Two.

# 1. *"Here's Another Fine Mess You've Gotten Me Into"*

Even if you've seen only a handful of the old Laurel and Hardy films, you'll probably recognize this immortal line, which the rotund Oliver Hardy would address to the wistful Stan Laurel whenever the boys found themselves hip-deep in still another misadventure. Hardy's ludicrous posturing and Laurel's teary-eyed consternation still tickle the funny bone and likely will for generations to come. Little wonder. We never cease to be amused by caricatures of natural human tendencies—in this case our penchant for self-depiction as innocent victims.

I think I initially suspected that we were fast becoming a nation of self-proclaimed victims in 1974, when I was writing my first book, an introductory college logic text. As an obvious example of faulty causal reasoning, I cited the curious case of an eighteen-year-old who was suing the San Francisco school system for $1 million because he had never learned to read or write, although he had graduated from one of that city's high schools. I observed that merely because the young man had passed through the San Francisco school system, his illiteracy intact, did not of itself establish the school system as the cause of his illiteracy. Indeed, because most of its graduates were literate, the blame would seem to lie with the student himself. Of course, a resourceful attorney might charge the school system with fraud if its diploma effectively guaranteed the student's literacy. But even then the "victim" himself would appear to be an accomplice to the fraud, for surely he must have known that he couldn't read or write when he so graciously accepted his diploma.

In any event, I chose the example because of its atypicality. (The uncommon, even bizarre example often provides a graceful entry into a complex topic like causation.) Little did I imagine that twenty years later what I was treating as a problem of logic would be a pervasive character disorder. I simply never anticipated that the ranks of such "victims" would swell until today we find ourselves awash in a sea of Mr. Hardys declaiming to all manner of Mr. Laurels: "Here's another fine mess you've gotten me into."

**NEWS ITEM:** A couple, run over by a train while making love on the subway tracks, sues the New York City Transit System.

**CHARGE:** The train company should have ensured the tracks were free of love-makers.

**NEWS ITEM:** A man hit by a car while riding his unlighted bicycle at night sues the bike's manufacturer.

**CHARGE:** The bike company should have posted a warning to the effect that it was dangerous to ride the bicycle unlighted at night.

**NEWS ITEM:** An elderly woman is burned by a cup of McDonald's coffee that splashes out of a paper cup she is attempting to open while holding it between her legs in a parked car. She sues McDonald's.

**CHARGE:** The coffee was too hot.

Similar examples, which could be multiplied manyfold, don't even include the category of "victimization by discrimination." With the proliferation of civil rights and disability acts, virtually all of us today—even an alcoholic transvestite—can find grounds for considering ourselves victims of one thing or another.

**NEWS ITEM:** The ABC news special that included the preceding cases also reported one about a Midwest school board that decided to fire its superintendent after the man, dressed as a woman, was busted for drunk driving. When the superintendent threatened to sue for discrimination against the disabled, the board paid him in excess of $100,000, plus his pension.

**NEWS ITEM:** In California, a man—after burglarizing a home, in which he tied up three victims and shot one in the head, blinding him—escapes with four guns and 250 rounds of ammunition. Police officers in pursuit, believing the burglar to be armed and dangerous, shoot him twice in the back as he tries to vault a six-foot fence into a neighboring yard. The man, who is serving a thirty-two-year prison sentence for the 1990 robbery, sues the four officers for violating his civil rights, because he was found to be unarmed at the time he was shot. A jury orders the officers each to pay the man $26,183, and the chief of police to pay him $80,000 in punitive damages.[1]

NEWS ITEM: A woman sues a city for issuing her a citation for snoring, after a neighbor who was being kept awake by the racket complains. After investigating the complaint at one thirty A.M., a noise enforcement officer fines the ear-splitting sleeper $50. Although the case is dismissed, the woman sues the city for $24,500, complaining of stress, humiliation, and lost wages as a result of the lawsuit. She settles for $13,500.[2]

Like the case of that high school graduate, it's tempting to write off such cases as anomalies. Perhaps they are, but only in degree, not type. In fact, cases like these represent a clearly discernible trend to blame others for what are largely the products of our own making. Sure, ill-conceived social policy, sophistic lawyers, mushy-headed judges, and overly sympathetic juries invite blame-shifting, thereby making self-blame seem naive, if not downright dumb. But the fact remains: The tendency to disconnect from the outcomes of our choices and conduct has taken grip and is played out every day in homely, unpublicized ways. Aggregately they represent a retreat from personal responsibility and often a papering over of basic character flaws: ignorance, stupidity, laziness, immoderation, imprudence, greed, self-absorption.

Not long ago I received a student essay that could hardly be read because it had been typed on a worn-out ribbon. When I refused to accept the paper, the shocked student informed me that she'd used one of the college's typewriters.

"Maybe so," I said to her, "but it's *your* paper, not the college's. Surely you're intelligent enough to observe a defective ribbon. Why didn't you do something about it?" She told me it was the college's responsibility to maintain its typewriters. "But it's *your* responsibility to turn in a readable paper," I reminded her. She stormed off, convinced, I suspect, that the college and I were at fault, not she.

A similar incident occurred in a speech class where a student found "totally unreasonable" the instructor's request that she turn off her pager while in class, because it was distracting and disturbing. "It's part of my job," she said before exiting the class with a threat of filing a grievance.

This student happened to be one of the legion of so-called "re-entry students" in our colleges today, individuals who are back in school after a hiatus to marry, have children, get divorced, fight an illness, join the army, rescue their families, go to work, or just plain play. Many of these individuals are mature, responsible adults who ask no academic quarter for the complexities of their lives, self-made or otherwise. They hold themselves fully accountable for their early-life decisions—for the jobs they must hold, the children they must support, and the basic skills they never mastered when they had the opportunity. Noteworthy among this exemplary group are individuals actively involved in recovery programs, where they're learning that the only real power they have—that any of us has—is the power to take full responsibility for their lives.

Unfortunately, however, there are too many "re-entries" who practice "victim manipulation." They pose as innocent victims, then attempt to milk the system. They variously expect and sometimes even demand that classes and curricula accommodate their personal needs, and that they be permitted to "challenge" classes, get credit for irrelevant work experience, be excused from class for work or family matters, or be allowed to bring their young children to class. In short, they want a college education, but on their terms—no matter that their terms sometimes amount to undeserved compensations for life circumstances of their own making. They don't see or won't admit that they're continuing the same pattern of responsibility avoidance that has left them desperately trying to make up for "lost time."

When it comes to personal health, you'll find no lack of Hardys looking for Laurels to blame for the messes they've largely gotten themselves into. Take cigarette smoking. Some of us would rather blame and sue tobacco companies than quit smoking. (In one case, the family of a late thirty-year chain smoker even went after the corner store where the deceased used to buy his cigarettes.)

Then there's the majority of us who overeat, underexercise, and mismanage stress—and by example are teaching our children to do the same. In other words, we're contributing mightily to our health problems and the next generation's. But rather than change, we ratchet up our demands on an already overburdened health care system. Instead of eating less and better, exercising more, and learning to manage our stress, we clamor for more drugs, better technology, and new surgical procedures. Then we blame bungling government, inefficient hospitals, greedy insurance and drug companies, and physicians, even illegal aliens—anybody but ourselves—for America's "health care crisis." Expecting medical science and government to rescue us from self-induced health problems is an unaffordable, infantile demand for risk-free self-indulgence.

What's the "red thread" running through these diverse cases? *A failure or refusal to identify with the outcomes of our choices and actions.* Instead of taking the heat, like Hardy we'd rather blame Laurel. But shifting the blame is not living like a mature adult, with conscious awareness of the possible and probable consequences of one's conduct. In fact, it's not really living at all, but more akin to sleepwalking through life.

Identifying with our actions and their outcomes requires consciousness of what we're doing, why, and what's at stake. For the 42 million smokers in the United States, for example, this means facing up to some harsh realities, and engaging in some tough "self-talk" like the following:

> I am fully aware of the enormous social costs and serious health consequences of smoking, which tobacco companies naturally will deny or downplay in order to make money. Nevertheless, I choose to run these risks and take full responsibility for the pleasure I get from smoking, even if it means the ravages of a fatal disease. I also recognize that this decision is mine and mine alone, and I have no right to impose the consequences of this decision on nonsmokers by subjecting them to the ill effects of *my* secondary smoke.

Again, those engaging in casual, unprotected sex need to have a "heart to heart" with themselves that goes something like this:

> I am aware of the high risk of contracting a sexually transmitted disease (STD) by engaging in promiscuous, unprotected sex. I also realize that on any given occasion I am having sex not only with some particular individual but with all individuals that that person has ever had sex with,

or will. I realize further that looks are deceiving; that "nice" people can harbor nasty diseases; that individuals often conceal, deceive, and even lie about their sexual history; that "love" will not protect me. I am also aware of the following facts about STDs: (1) STDs are flourishing in the United States. (2) Young adults are the primary casualties. (3) STDs boost the risk of contracting human immunodeficiency virus (HIV), which is associated with AIDS, becoming infertile, or giving birth to babies with health problems. (4) STDs often attack women silently, without symptoms. (5) Some STDs—notably genital herpes and HIV—are at present incurable. With full awareness of the preceding, I take total responsibility for the pleasure of engaging in promiscuous or unprotected sex, even if it means contracting or transmitting a lifelong, perhaps fatal disease that may jeopardize or even preclude my future relationships and plans, for example, marriage and family.

———•◆•———

The failure of an Oliver Hardy is that he never learns. He never develops any self-awareness, any insight into his own complicity in the messes he finds himself in. On the screen this is amusing. In real life it's pitiable, and sometimes tragic.

# 2. *"Don't Blame Me, I Didn't Vote for Him / Her"*

As an expressway expression of human immaturity, this popular bumper sticker is hard to beat. A political play on Hardy's complaint, it announces to the motoring public that the driver accepts no responsibility for the perceived mess of things being created by some recently elected official and the suckers who voted for him or her. It says, "I'm an innocent victim being held hostage by an evil regime."

The individuals who brandish such signs probably mistake the exposure of error for the discovery of truth, for the more the new incumbent falters and stumbles, the more these sore losers crow, "I told you so." Evidently, nothing could please them more than for the wicked winners to fail miserably. Then the forces of light and truth may once more reign. Never mind that no sooner will that happy day arrive than "Don't blame me" will appear on a different fleet of vehicles piloted by the latest self-proclaimed hostage-victims. And so it goes, the careening from one election to the next, aided with gusto by the few who profit from the passions of the party and the madness of the multitude.

In general, political bumper stickers give truth to Henry Adams's opinion of politics. "Politics as a practice," said the esteemed American historian and scholar in his famous autobiography, ". . . [has] always been the systematic organization of hatreds."[1] "Don't blame me" certainly leaves no doubt about who and what are disliked and disdained. It instantly tags the villain, the dark and sinister source of all our problems. It tells not only whom but what to hate: ambiguity, complexity, nuance—in other words, reality. Political bumper stickers are for those who can't stand very much reality—those who prefer a fantasy world of moral absolutes and dualisms, of instantly identifiable allies and adversaries, friends and enemies, good and evil. The world of the politicized bumper is a monochromatic world without subtlety or shade, inhabited by mutually exclusive camps of knee-jerk cynics locked in unending power struggles. Power and control—that's basically what "Don't blame me" is all about, not the public good and responsible citizenship. And because power grabbing works best if disguised as righteous entitlement and victimization, bumper politics usually reflects a false sense of one's essential innocence and goodness in relation to others, and, therefore, superiority to them.

"A nation gets the government it deserves." Unlike "Don't blame me," there's no false innocence or superiority in this square-shouldered expression, no unearned entitlement or disguised power lust—just the blunt truth. It says: If government is too big, perhaps it's because *all* of us, in some way or other, expect too much of it. If it's inefficient, perhaps it's because we're paying too many others to do what too few of us are willing to do for ourselves. If it's overly regulatory, perhaps it's because we lack self-control. If it's unresponsive, perhaps it's because we're unresponsive to the common good. If it's wasteful, perhaps it's because we're greedy. If it's run by too many lawyers, perhaps it's because we've made litigation a national blood sport. If it's corrupt, perhaps it's because we'd rather be rich than right. In short, if, as H. L. Mencken said, "Under democracy one party always devotes its chief energies to trying to prove that the other party is unfit to rule—and both commonly succeed and are right,"[2] perhaps it's because that's exactly what we want. "Don't blame me" certainly points in that direction.

Is it any wonder that office seekers and their minions spend millions feeding our fears, stoking our hatreds, and making piecrust promises, when we seek miracle workers and messiahs, not mere mortals like ourselves? But caped heroes are the stuff of comic books and fantasy films, not real life. The action hero of the latest cinematic blockbuster is the alter ego of the self-absorbed adolescent, not the mature adult. The people we elect cannot rescue us; they can only represent us. And they can do that honestly only if we're honest with ourselves. Basic to that honesty is acknowledging that government—any government—is highly flawed. Montaigne was right when he wrote: "It is very easy to accuse a government of imperfection, for all mortal things are full of it."[3]

Governance today is especially inexpedient because we have made it the principal expedient. Like spoiled children incessantly ratcheting up demands on their parents, we expect government to do everything. The less government we say we want is always less for the other guy, rarely for ourselves. But government can't and shouldn't do every-thing. And what it can and should do doesn't come pain-free or with a money-back guarantee if not satisfied. No party or personality can make us smarter, better, freer, richer, or healthier than we want to be. If we think it can, we deserve the party and personality we get.

Teddy Roosevelt said that "the first requisite of a good citizen in this republic of ours is that he shall be able and willing to pull his weight."[4] Pulling our weight, our twenty-sixth president explained, isn't only "the capacity for sturdy self-help" but also "self-respecting regard for the rights of others." When one has no immediate stake in an outcome, it's easy to disrespect ourselves by disregarding the rights of others. It's easy for me, for example, to take no responsibility for public transportation because I never take the bus. It's similarly easy for owners of beachfront or mountain property to blithely ignore responsibilities with respect to recreational commons; for those with health insurance to ignore those without it; for families who live in superior school districts to benignly neglect those in inferior ones. When we deliberately squelch the legitimate interests of those attempting to secure the very things we cherish— education, health care and security, equal treatment, mobility, recreational opportunities—we are not only *not* carrying our weight, we are adding to the weight of others.

As for the losers of elections, they're not entitled to be mere passengers—or ones who merely rock the boat. They, too, must carry their weight. Given the tendency to place party first, we're most inclined to pervert the Roosevelt doctrine of "sturdy self-help" and "self-respecting regard for the rights of others" when our side loses and is out of power. It's then—as we overidentify with party, personality, issue, or ideology—that we're inclined to pervert the role of the "loyal opposition" into political guerrilla warfare. It's then that we're tempted to snipe, subvert, and sabotage the ruling party by marginalizing its successes and exaggerating its failures, all in preparation for the triumphant arrival of the next new-and-improved politician-product freshly minted on the presses of image makers. And while we're eagerly awaiting the advent of the latest and greatest savior, we do our damnedest to safeguard our own narrow interests. We work hard and spend much to block any changes made at our personal expense. We dispatch legions of mercenaries—euphemistically called "lobbyists" and "political action committees"—to seats of power to protect our pork. We cajole and strong-arm elected officials to vote our way or hit the highway. And then, when little gets done and problems worsen, we gripe about "congressional gridlock" and rail against a weak, wicked, wasteful government. Mad as hell and unwilling to take it anymore, we give the boot to one set of government-sapping interest groups and the glad hand to another—our own.

———•◆•———

Nowadays, when I find myself idling behind some Oliver Hardy complaining "Don't blame me, I didn't vote for him," in my mind's eye I see the wise words of Walt Kelly, creator of *Pogo:* "We has met the enemy, and it is us."

# 3. "I Didn't Want to Get Involved"

Remember Kitty Genovese? She was the young woman who was repeatedly stabbed by her killer in a half-hour attack that occurred in front of her New York apartment while thirty-eight neighbors looked, listened, and did nothing, not even call the police. They didn't want to get involved. Apparently neither did at least forty people who witnessed the brutal attack on Deletha Word, 31, the 5-foot, 115-pound woman who leaped to her death off a bridge in Detroit after 6-foot-4, 260-pound Mantel Welch, 20, stripped and beat her savagely, and chased her with a tire iron. (When found guilty of second-degree murder, Welch blamed the media for his conviction.)

If onlookers like these symbolize bystander apathy, then T. J. Murphy and Tee Bennett symbolize care and concern. Murphy and Bennett are the two African-American men who braved a mob's savagery to save a white truck driver. As aptly chronicled, Reginald Denny was the wrong color in the wrong place at the wrong time.[1] The thirty-six-year-old father of two was attempting to inch his twenty-seven-ton load of gravel through an angry knot of mostly black people protesting the 1992 acquittal of four Los Angeles police officers charged with using excessive force in the arrest of African-American Rodney King, when he was dragged from his cab and beaten with gusto by six men.

Like thousands of other viewers, Murphy and Bennett, both unemployed at the time, witnessed the ugly incident on a TV screen. They watched as Denny was punched repeatedly in the face and abdomen, and collapsed in the street only to be kicked in the head until, covered with blood, he stopped moving. One young black male later was quoted as saying: "Rodney King was the white man's verdict; that guy in the semi was our verdict."[2] But unlike King, whom a videotape showed being beaten by police, Denny was rescued. So appalled were they by what they were witnessing that Murphy and Bennett rushed out to help the truck driver. "We said to each other, 'Somebody got to get that guy out of there,' " Murphy was reported saying afterward. "It was just like Rodney King. They beat him and they beat him."[3]

Moved by what they saw, the two men drove three blocks to the scene. When the street became clogged with cars, they set out on foot. They found that Denny, whom the mob had abandoned, had regained consciousness and managed to crawl back into the cab. He was slumped over the wheel, his head badly swollen. Two other Good Samaritans joined Murphy and Bennett in the cab, and together they steered the big rig away from the scene to a nearby hospital. Another person, a white woman, drove in front of the truck blaring her horn and flashing emergency lights to clear the way to the emergency room. Although it took months, Denny made a remarkable recovery.

It's not always easy to get involved. When what we perceive as our own self-interest, let alone our safety, is at risk, our natural tendency is to turn away. We're also naturally inclined to exaggerate the personal costs of involvement. Then there's the group-size factor: The larger the group we're members of, the less personal responsibility we tend to feel. So we almost always can find an excuse for noninvolvement. But mere inconvenience, irrational fear, or common cowardice aren't good reasons to downplay or play dumb to someone else's pain and suffering. Neither is an easy but baseless assumption that somebody else is taking appropriate action. In brief, no one is expected to be a hero, but everyone is required to meet the minimal expressions of human decency, caring, and concern.

The biblical injunction to love one's neighbor as oneself stands in opposition to the glib "I don't want to get involved." The former recognizes the social aspect of living that the latter ignores or rejects. But often we define *neighbor* too narrowly. In this respect many of us differ little from "homeboys" and "homegirls"—fiercely loyal to clan and chillingly indifferent to anyone else. Like the gang member's, our conception of neighbor and grounds for involvement often is restricted to family and friends. It can differ little from the racist's, who—one philosopher observes—restricts neighborly concern to members of his own race; or from the nationalist's, who finds the limit of neighborly concern at the borders of her own nation.[4]

Juxtaposed to these ingrown conceptions of neighbor and involvement are those of individuals like Murphy and Bennett, who didn't even know Denny and had no obvious obligation to endanger themselves by assisting him. Like thousands of others who watched the grisly scene on TV, Murphy and Bennett could have sat, stared, and done nothing. They could have played dumb. Instead, they realized Denny's existence in a wholly different way—they identified with him. His danger became their danger, his pain theirs. They had what philosopher William Frankena calls "a more perfect recognition of our neighbors"[5]—that is, as individuals who are fundamentally like ourselves. "We ought, all of us, to realize each other in this intense, pathetic, and important way," says Frankena, quoting William James.[6]

It was their capacity to feel what Denny was feeling that affected Murphy and Bennett's conduct toward him. "Somebody got to get that guy out of there," they said. And then, rather than shifting the responsibility to someone else, they in effect asked, "Why shouldn't it be me?" Murphy and Bennett thus showed the same concern for Reginald Denny's well-being as they naturally would for their own. To show a like concern for others as for self is at the heart of personal involvement and responsibility.

The Scottish philosopher David Hume interpreted concern for others as compassion or sympathy. Sympathy is how Hume thought we make moral distinctions. It's a sentiment we feel not only toward other persons but all pain-feeling beings. More than just a feeling we might have for someone who has suffered a loss, sympathy is the means by which we feel what the person is feeling. It's our capacity to make the pain of others our own pain, what we today call "empathy."

Like any other capacity, empathy can be developed or not. It's up to each of us. In some individuals—Mother Teresa, for example—it appears extraordinarily honed. In others— Hitler comes to mind—it seems nonexistent. Murphy and Bennett exhibited sympathy, Kitty Genovese's neighbors and Deletha Word's onlookers did not. Murphy and Bennett felt Denny's pain and danger, however superficially different Denny was from them. They shone with that "spark of friendship for human kind" and that "particle of the dove" Hume said was "kneaded into our frame."[7] They exhibited what Rollo May called "perceptual courage," the "capacity to *perceive,* to let one's self see the suffering of other people." "If we let ourselves experience the evil," wrote the famous existential therapist in *The Courage to Create:*

> we will be forced to do something about it. It is a truth rec-
> ognizable in all of us, that when we don't want to become
> involved, when we don't want to confront *even* the issue of
> whether or not we'll come to the aid of someone who is
> being unjustly treated, we block perception, we blind our-
> selves to the other's suffering, we cut off our empathy with
> the person needing help. Hence the most prevalent form of
> cowardice in our day hides behind the statement: I did not
> want to become involved.[8]

———— • ◆ • ————

Getting involved is often inconvenient, sometimes imprudent, and occasionally risky. But the alternative— practiced indifference—leaves undeveloped the human in us: compassion, care, concern. A habitual refusal to get involved is the equivalent of not wanting to be a mature, responsible adult, which is to say: "I won't grow up. I don't want to grow up."

# 4. *"How Was I Supposed to Know?"*

A chronically absent student once questioned a C grade I'd given him. He figured that his 79 percent average was close enough to 80, the minimum for a B. I explained that if he had attended class more faithfully and participated more actively, I'd have cut him some slack. "Unfortunately," I said, "you gave me no reason to bump you up a grade." With righteous indignation he replied, "But how was I supposed to know attendance and participation count?"

My syllabus lengthens with the years. What once consisted mainly of a course outline and grade requirements now contains policies about attendance, punctuality, and participation—they all count. Broad policy statements need spelling out for the benefit of the increasing number of "loopholers." Thus, "Leaving class after the role is taken *does not mean* you were present for the class . . . there are no 'excused absences.' Like a rose, an absence is an absence is an absence." Actually, I'm rather generous with absences, permitting somewhat more than institutional policy before dropping a student from a class. My sufferance is not altogether selfless, however. I prefer to keep my answering machine free of tales of colds and cramps, of car crashes and court appearances, of deaths and dyings and other wretched fates. It doesn't work, of course. The calls keep coming and the tape keeps running. I suppose I should record a new outgoing message stipulating the kinds of messages that under no circumstances are to be left at the sound of the tone.

Simple rules of classroom etiquette can't be assumed. Many students, for example, need to be reminded that class concludes at the appointed hour, not ten minutes earlier, as signaled by their shuffling and packing up. I'm currently drafting a "grazing policy": "Keep in mind that you're in a classroom, not at the movies. If you *must* snack—for example, you're hypoglycemic—please deposit cans, containers, and cartons in the wastebasket before leaving, and wipe up all spills." I'm also contemplating a no-hat policy, and flunking the next student who asks me, "Are we going to do anything important today?" Of course, I'd publicize the latter first; otherwise someone would complain: "How was I supposed to know you'd flunk me for asking, 'Are we going to do anything important today?'" Such a person would be the same kind who doesn't get, misplaces, or loses the syllabus to begin with, and because of whom I now periodically announce: "It is your responsibility to have, understand, and comply with the course syllabus." (I dread the day someone bleats on my answering machine, "I wasn't in class when you said that about the syllabus.")

When that student asked me how he was supposed to know that attendance and participation count, I told him he should have assumed so, or at least not presumed otherwise. I suggested, perhaps futilely, that he might give some thought to what it means to be a student enrolled in a class. If he did, he might realize that, among other things, it ordinarily means regular attendance and involvement. When an individual is faithful to the classes and actively engaged in their ongoing activities, he's acting as a student is supposed to act. When he isn't, he's not. How do we know all this? By knowing what a student is. By inquiring into what it means to be a student. By distinguishing the role of a student from other roles and activities. Absent that, we lose or blur important distinctions between a student, on the one hand, and, say, a moviegoer or a parent, on the other. Studying, moviegoing, and parenting are different activities that entail different duties and behaviors. Mature people make role distinctions and sort out responsibilities. Reflecting on the nature and function of our roles helps us know in general what we're supposed to do and how we're supposed to act.

The pitiful reality is that many of us—like some students—have come to believe that we need to be told everything; and, worse, that if we aren't, we're excusably ignorant. But ignorance of minimal, commonsense expectations of our roles, activities, and practices is no excuse. It's mindlessness or laziness, perhaps; avoidance of blame, probably; a self-serving cop-out, almost certainly. But a good excuse? Hardly.

Why do we keep ourselves ignorant? One reason is to avoid having to face or do something distasteful. The wife who won't acknowledge her husband's incest or battering. The father who studiously avoids knowing his child's friends or whereabouts. The chain smoker who insists that cigarettes don't really kill. Making life changes, confronting evil, dealing with shame, enforcing discipline—none of this is easy. Who wouldn't rather avoid it? And what more expedient way than playing ostrich; and then, when the truth seeps out (as it usually does) casting oneself as innocently ignorant? "How was I supposed to know my husband was incesting my daughter?" "How was I supposed to know my child was keeping bad company?" Knowing such things is part of what being a spouse and a parent is all about—a good one, at any rate.

Other times we play dumb in order to maintain a belief, even if it's a lie. We can so want something to be the case that we ignore, dismiss, or warp any counterinformation. Some individuals, for example, so much want to believe that their family is perfect that they don't or won't even notice some of its serious imperfections. They probably have given no more thought to the nature of a family, any family, than the average churchgoer has given to the nature of religion, any religion. If they had, they might permit themselves to know that the notion of family perfection they seek to maintain is pure fantasy; that all families, like all individuals, are strong in some ways, weak in others— sometimes outstanding, other times outrageous. Rather than disturbing, such knowledge can be profoundly comforting and strengthening. It can allow us to embrace our families—warts and all—and ourselves as well.

Still other times our self-imposed ignorance gives us a kind of license to do what we want to do but perhaps shouldn't. Remember that couple who were run over by the train while gamboling on the tracks? They blamed the transit company for the mess they got themselves into, and excused themselves by reason of ignorance. How were they supposed to know a train might come trundling down, of all places, the tracks of a subway tunnel?

And how were the hosts supposed to know when they invited Don Imus to speak at their annual Radio & Television Correspondents Association Dinner in 1996 that the radio jock would crudely insult President Clinton and the first lady, both of whom sat only a few feet away? How could the committee possibly have suspected that the irreverent shock jock, notorious for smirking insider jokes and gossip, could possibly turn in so raunchy a performance that its chairperson— also vice president of programming at C-SPAN—would have to send a letter of "apology" to the Clintons? Well, it was technically an apology. "To apologize," said Ambrose Bierce, "is to lay the foundation for a future offense."[1] Two days later C-SPAN rebroadcast the entire program.

Speaking of having the guest for dinner, what about the riotous ruse those *Jenny Jones* cutups pulled on still another dupe for a day? It seems that Jonathan Schmitz, a twenty-four-year-old man, had arrived to tape a segment of the syndicated TV talk show with the understanding that he'd be meeting a "secret admirer." Much to Schmitz's surprise, his secret admirer turned out to be not a female, as Schmitz had assumed, but thirty-one-year-old Scott Amedure. The show was actually about men who had crushes on other men. Schmitz told the audience he was straight, and he maintained his composure throughout the show. Inside, however, he apparently felt embarrassed, and two days later he shot and killed his "secret admirer," Scott Amedure.

Donna Kelly, the female friend of Schmitz's who, together with Amedure and show officials, had persuaded Schmitz to go on the show, expressed shock at the murder. It was all in fun, she said. The show's producers also expressed disbelief and sadness, and decided not to air the segment. Two months before, in an interview with the *New York Daily News*, host Jenny Jones was quoted as saying that she and the producers had made a conscious decision two years earlier not to do sleazy topics. "We try to use a little restraint," she said.[2]

Now, the most natural thing in the world is for Kelly and show officials to disown any responsibility for this tragedy with the stock, "How was I supposed to know that Schmitz would wig out and kill somebody?" Fair enough. But shouldn't they have known—or at least considered—that they were setting Schmitz up to be exposed and embarrassed on national television? that one party's fun and profit is another's public humiliation? that public shame can be incendiary; that without knowing Schmitz's personality—notably his feelings about homosexuality and potential for violence—they could not predict, let alone control events? that public humiliation for fun and profit is a base business?[3]

And how were Kelly and the *Jenny Jones* mirth-makers (and even Amedure) supposed to know that in these respects the "gun" was loaded? By giving serious thought to what it means to be a friend and a decent human being. Had they, they'd have thought twice about ambushing Schmitz, or setting up any other person for public humiliation.

Of course, Schmitz is no innocent in the whole sleazy affair. What did he think the *Jenny Jones* show was, a match-making service? Shouldn't he have known, or found out, that daytime talk shows like *Jenny Jones* feast off the embarrassment and humiliation of "guests" by exposing the most intimate details of their lives, then taping their reactions for the titillation of audiences, who themselves take no blame for what happens?

In brief, the respective agendas of all parties—ratings and profit for the show; fun and perhaps notoriety for Kelly; an admirer and possibly fifteen minutes of fame for Schmitz and Amedure; crass amusement for the TV audience—conveniently masked the darker side of what was transpiring, and the complicity of all in it. They believed and did exactly what they preferred to, and afterward asked, "But how was I supposed to know?" (The Amedure family subsequently slapped the *Jenny Jones* show and its producer, Warner Bros., with a $25 million lawsuit, arguing that the defendants were directly responsible for Schmitz's conduct in that their own conduct instigated the slaying. A spokesperson for the Libel Defense Resource Center in New York said the lawsuit defied common sense because "It presumes humans aren't responsible for their own actions."[4])

The same reasons that motivate individuals to practice ignorance also motivate groups of individuals. Corporations, political parties, presidential administrations, police departments, legislative and ecclesiastical bodies, all have their particular slants on things, which they will strive to protect and preserve at almost any cost. Keeping themselves comfortably in the dark is an expedient way for key personnel to avoid tough but right decisions, push the group's agenda, and cut moral corners. At the upper levels of business and government—institutions and organizations of all sorts—many individuals work hard at not getting hurt by not knowing too much. This is variously termed "being insulated," "out of the loop," or "plausible deniability." By any other name, buzzwords all for "How was I supposed to know?" Unfortunately, it isn't often enough that such vacuous utterances are met with a resounding: "You should have known! It's your job to know! Now own up!" Perhaps it's because those who should be saying that—you and I—are too busy saying, "How was I supposed to know?"

————•◆•————

"What you don't know can't hurt you" goes the expression. Perhaps so. But an ancient Arabic apothegm says that those who know not are either foolish or simple. If the former, they should be shunned; if the latter, taught. In either case, then, a comfort that flows from ignorance is best received like cold porridge.[5]

# 5. *"It's Not in My Job Description"*

If you grew up in a home where household chores were assigned, you may remember occasionally being asked to do something that was not, strictly speaking, one of your jobs. You obeyed, but perhaps uncheerfully. After all, taking out the trash was your brother or sister's job, not yours. That neither was available probably mattered little, and certainly didn't alter the fact that your chores included dog walking and car washing, but definitely not trash removal and lawn mowing.

Holding children accountable for household chores that they've been assigned and taught how to do is a time-honored way to instill a sense of responsibility in them. But sometimes children can overidentify with a particular responsibility— for example, taking care of their rooms—and play dumb to the more general one of which it's a specification: keeping the *house* clean and neat. Hence the child who strolls around the mounting kitchen garbage because "It's not my job to take out the trash." So, while a division of labor can be an efficient way to meet household needs, it can also obscure the general responsibilities of all family members, regardless of their particular assignments. The same holds true in the work world.

Not long ago I was in a popular local coffeehouse and noticed a spill near the entrance. When I brought it to the attention of the idle clerk, she shouted in the direction of the kitchen for assistance. Minutes passed, the clerk continued to dawdle, and the spill went untended. Finally, I decided to dab it up with some napkins. But before I could start, the clerk called me off with, "Oh, don't worry about that. We'll take care of it." Then she barked toward the kitchen again for "a hand out here." Eventually a sweaty and bedraggled figure emerged with a mop large enough to tar a roof. With one deft swab, he made the pool vanish. But he couldn't conceal his annoyance with the impassive clerk. As he returned to the kitchen, he hurled some uncharitable remark her way. "Well, that's not *my* job!" she fired back. I couldn't help wondering whether she thought general neatness and safety were her job, not to mention protecting the business against lawsuits.

It's not surprising that many of us are more versed in the letter of our jobs than in their spirit. Too often in the past, employers have made excessive demands of time and performance on employees and set expectations that well exceeded what the individuals were hired to do. The abominable work conditions that gave rise to labor unions are well documented. So are organized labor's laudable goals of worker protection and empowerment, which are specifications of two high moral ideals: noninjury and individual autonomy.

On the other hand, as the work world becomes increasingly polarized along labor-management lines, workers tend to define their responsibilities strictly by the letter of the job description or agreement, and sometimes even seem compelled to by collective bargaining arrangements. The upshot frequently is a contraction of individual responsibility to the narrowest interpretation of what one is getting paid to do, and not a scintilla more.

But job descriptions never mention that, within the limits of law and ethics, all employees are expected to act on behalf of the employer in carrying out their jobs. Ideally, then, the mature employee is mindful of some maxim like: "Act in a way that you would want your employees to act were you their employer." (By the same token, mature and responsible employers treat their employees as they would want to be treated were they the employees.)

This workers' "Golden Rule" of the workplace provides a useful guideline for what we as employees should always refrain from doing, on the one hand, and what we sometimes should be doing, on the other. In other words, it flushes out negative and positive obligations. On the negative side, workers who follow this rule would never deliberately subordinate the welfare of the business to their personal gain, convenience, or pleasure. For example, they wouldn't take paid sick days for fun in the sun, or clock in a tardy coworker. Supervisors would never use subordinates for personal matters, and key officials would never exploit inside information for personal advantage or rip off a trade secret. On the positive side, employees would give serious thought to a variety of workplace-honoring actions, from reporting the in-house thief to the one filing a fraudulent worker's compensation claim.

None of this is intended to oversimplify the moral dilemmas that today's worker can face. And it certainly doesn't mean that workers *always* owe first allegiance to their employers. Yes, workers owe their employers loyalty, but not to the point of lying to, harming, or treating others unfairly. The point is that the job description or work agreement doesn't address these matters of ordinary morality and responsibility that are owed a variety of individuals—from fellow workers, customers, and competitors to government and the broader society—any more than the ones owed to employers.

In the professions, specialization heightens the tendency to view workplace responsibility solely through the lens of the job description, and thus to play dumb to whatever lies outside it. The more specialized we become, the narrower our field of vision tends to be. Philosopher Michael Davis calls this narrowing of consciousness "microscopic vision," which he defines as "enhanced vision or giving up of information not likely to be useful under the circumstances for information more likely to be useful."[1] Microscopic vision, says Davis, is a power. It enables the specialist to discern what the untrained eye or ear cannot. But, though microscopic vision is vital to an array of activities from gardening to brain surgery, it has a price: "You cannot both look into the microscope and see what you would see if you did not." If the specialist never looks up from the microscope, she will lose the ability to see the world as ordinary people do, as well as the ethical dimensions of what she's doing. As a case in point, Davis cites events surrounding the fateful launch of the space shuttle *Challenger*.

You may recall that on the eve of the launch, technicians at Morton Thiokol, including Vice President for Engineering Robert Lund, unanimously recommended against a launch, on the basis of previous flight data that near-freezing temperatures would erode the O-rings, causing the shuttle to explode. Eager to launch, officials at the space center urged Thiokol engineers to reconsider. Lund was specifically told to "take off [your] engineering hat and put on [your] management hat," that is, to view the decision from the perspective of a schedule-conscious manager, not a safety-conscious engineer. Viewing the launch as an ordinary management decision, Lund the manager (versus Lund the engineer) could rationally justify the potential risk for the potential benefit. So he changed his mind. The *Challenger* was launched the next morning and exploded minutes after liftoff when the O-rings failed, killing all aboard.

———•◆•———

The specific responsibilities one assumes with a job—whether it's taking out the household trash, cleaning up a restaurant coffee spill, or launching a spacecraft—certainly affect the strength of one's obligations. But they don't exhaust them. What is *not* in our job descriptions may be precisely what we ought to do, and what *is* in them may be precisely what we ought *not* do. Part of being a mature, responsible adult is recognizing the difference and making the distinctions, not playing dumb to them.

# 6. *"The Computer Is Down"*

Hardly computer fluent, I'm not exactly sure why the teller can't tell me the balance of my checking account because, as she says, "The computer is down." Called by some "one of the most feared expressions of modern times," friends report hearing "the computer is down" in other contexts: making reservations, tracking bills, obtaining credit information, even trading stock. One calls it a "belch in the system."

"Down" computers may be just a bump along the information superhighway, but they're pause-giving nevertheless. One wonders why it is that a customer can't get an account balance because "the computer is down." Or more to the point: Why wouldn't a teller find such a development at least mildly peculiar? After all, isn't account information as basic a responsibility as a financial institution has? Isn't making reservations what hotel clerks do? Aren't ticket agents supposed to sell tickets? Perhaps if I knew more about the idiosyncrasies of computers I wouldn't find any of this odd. And maybe I wouldn't be as cowed by the teller when she says, "The computer is down." I might intelligently challenge her, instead of merely slouching toward the exits with all the stoic resignation of a fan who's been told the game's been called because of rain.

The frustration of not instantly getting what we want is something few of us entirely outgrow, but probably should. So being stiffed by a computer does have its merits. It can teach patience, a handful of which, goes a proverb, is better than a bushel of brains. But while we're learning to be more Job-like waiting for the down computer to "get up," we might ponder our relationship to technology.

"He that invents a machine," gushed writer and cleric Henry W. Beecher in the nineteenth century, "augments the power of a man and the well-being of mankind."[1] Viewing technology as no more than a complex tool—an extension of the human hand, as it were—has always inspired Beecher-like paeans to mechanical invention. But another Henry, and a contemporary of Beecher's, was less impressed with the power machines confer than the bondage they impose. "Men have become tools of their tools," Henry David Thoreau said in *Walden*.[2] A century later Erich Fromm would update the naturalist's dismal verdict of the machine. Observing that "the danger of the past was that men became slaves," the renowned student of social conditioning in human behavior warned that "the danger of the future is that men may become robots."[3]

A robot functions mechanically, without original thought. It's neither self-governing nor morally sensible. What it can and does do is respond to commands, which it follows automatically. In this sense humans can act robotically, and this was Fromm's fear.

But we also mimic robots in our relations with our inventions, as when we become so dependent on them that we almost can't function without them. Then what's intended to empower disempowers, what should give control takes it, and what arranges our lives keeps us from experiencing them. When this happens, it's easy to forget who's in charge. We humans are, of course, not our machines; it's we who are ultimately accountable. But a stiffened dependency slackens self-reliance, and subtly shifts the locus of responsibility from human to machine. Then who is to blame for not having the account balance? Not us, but our computers—which is like blaming the rain for the game's cancellation. "The computer is down" can, thus, become a socially acceptable excuse for disowning some very basic responsibilities—a high-tech version of "The dog ate my homework."

Perhaps this point can be made with another example, mind-numbing but true. A student submitted a perfectly formatted paper studded with eye-fetching, multicolored graphics—in all a compelling example of the marvels of the modern personal computer. This mechanized tour de force was also unorganized, incoherent, and riddled with faulty diction and misspellings, all of which puzzled its author when his attention was drawn to it. How could this be when his WordPerfect program had assured accuracy? A friendly reminder about the iron-clad law of GIGO—garbage in, garbage out—left him unfazed. He just mumbled something about getting better software. For this student, the problem and its solution lay not with him, but computer software. So did the blame. I imagined him storming home to kick the computer-dog who had devoured his homework.

Actually, personifying computers, as this student seemed to do, isn't that unusual. Research in communications and social psychology finds that we respond to PCs and computers as humans. We get mad at them, praise them, scream and swear at them, and even accuse them of cheating at games. In short, we treat computers like social beings and are encouraged to by manufacturers turning out software products that use a "social interface," that is, making computers adhere to "social norms."[4]

The friendlier computers become, the more of us want to make them our friends, companions, teachers, guides, gurus, matchmakers, entertainers, and social directors. Falling for clever, tough advertising, millions of us are rushing out pell-mell to purchase computers and get on-line, often not knowing why.[5] That the technology is new and different is reason enough for many to believe that it will make them and their children smarter and more competitive. But what's new and different isn't necessarily better. "Progress through technology" often sounds better than it plays.

Not long ago a Microsoft ad featured two little girls asking their father to forgo "Goldilocks" as their bedtime story and instead use the household computer to explain Sartre and existentialism. It's easy to imagine affluent parents snapping at this bait, and the less well-off regretting, perhaps even feeling guilty, that they can't afford to. It's far more difficult, though, to imagine many moms and dads thinking critically about what the ad is implying about learning and parenting.

In a masterstroke of irony, this ad debunked the fairy tale, which is a tried and true way to make complex issues palatable to young, unformed minds—*existential* issues like freedom, choice, and responsibility. The ad also downplayed the emotional and educational value of parents' reading to their children, and may even be suggesting, without foundation, that children who learn on multimedia computers do better in school than kids who stick to books.

Choosing and using any technology is tricky business. With everything from automobiles and pharmaceuticals to nuclear power and superconductivity, benefits always cost. If we're careless, we can be so dazzled by the vaunted "upside potential" that we miss the inevitable downside risks. We can end up being self-indulgent, for example, where self-control is in order—thus individuals who use cholesterol-reducing drugs as license to binge or those who use condoms as a warrant for "safe" promiscuous sex, or drivers who treat airbags and shoulder straps as permits to drive less defensively or ones who use their cellular phones as lethal extensions of their offices. We can also become so enamored of technology that we neglect the true nature of a problem and its solution, as that student did; or as millions of public school teachers do who rank "computer literacy" more important than the classics in a child's education. Or a physician does when she's mentally rifling through her arsenal of drugs rather than listening intently to what a patient is saying or not saying that may indicate a *non*medical condition. (By the same token, patients might ask themselves how satisfied they are to leave a doctor's office without a prescription in hand. I, for one, feel cheated. A true child of the Enlightenment, I want that little white paper with Latin squiggles on it that promises a quick fix for what ails me—whether or not I need it.)

Computers are no different from other technologies in this respect. Like drugs and car phones, they too have the capacity to impart a false security and power, which are natural setups for imprudence, delusion, and error.

For those who can afford them, computers and on-line services offer an emporium of information, ideas, and activities. They can bring together people whose paths never would have crossed. But there's also plenty of junk in cyberspace: trivia that passes for news, name-calling for rational argument, gibberish for art. Conversations in "chat rooms" aren't the same as "real" human interactions, and not all easy-to-access information is worth accessing, let alone storing in our heads as if they were vaults for trivia and "factoids." In brief, as internet enthusiast Howard Rheingold has pointed out, it's easy to confuse the tools with the task, computer networks with citizenship and building community.[6]

Then there's the darkly seductive side of electronic technology—the world of "players" hunched over the glowing computer screen for forty, fifty, even eighty hours a week, some stealing time from jobs, classes, and families.[7] And there's the world of the naive and lonely net surfer drawn by the siren call of some faceless predator promising fun and freedom. Consider Tara Noble, for example, the girl lured away from her Kentucky home to the streets of southern California by an e-mail sent by someone named George over the America Online computer network. "It's not what you think it is," the thirteen-year-old said after turning up on Hollywood Boulevard, two weeks older and years wiser. "They want one thing. They want you."[8] Tara, of course, was referring to on-line prowlers. But hers is a cautionary tale about careless and casual deployment of the PC and other technology in the home. Eternal vigilance, it seems, is as much the price of household technology as of liberty.

But vigilance isn't easy up against technology's promise of ever more freedom and prosperity, of power and security. Cutting-edge electronics is the "latest song," which the poet Homer said always gets the most applause. It's "here and now," "new and different," "bigger and better." Few want to be left behind with the old and "useless" when an orgiastic future is at their push-button fingertips. But that's all the more reason for vigilance, skepticism, and suspended belief. Having critical vision to anticipate its downside is a responsibility of owning all household technology. And respecting their dark potential is the only way to avoid excusing ourselves by blaming our inventions.

———•◆•———

There are, perhaps, good reasons that "the computer is down." But a down computer isn't a good reason for a bank holiday.

# 7. "But I Thought You Were on the Pill!"

In her best-seller *How Could You Do That?!*, Dr. Laura Schlessinger writes about a twenty-year-old caller named Michael who, the radio host says, "was facing doing right after being wronged."[1] It seems that for nearly a year Michael had been having a sexual relationship with a young woman whom he'd told he didn't want children. The woman had been taking birth-control pills, but about seven months earlier had stopped without informing Michael. Now she was pregnant. "I feel she did it to keep me in her life," he says. "She told some friends that she knew of situations like this where the father eventually came around and they lived happily ever after. I feel responsible for the kid, but don't know what to do because I'm so angry with her."[2]

One reason it's so easy to shift blame is that it's just as easy to believe what we want to believe. Perhaps in no area more than sexual conduct are these twin tendencies more pronounced. Then and there, when passion overwhelms reason, our preferred beliefs can permit us to do what we want and afterward play dumb to what we really should have known.

When men like Michael feel tricked and in effect protest to women they've impregnated, "But I thought you were on the pill!" they're expressing an irrational belief in risk-free, pregnancy-proof sex, and using that ignorance to escape blame. And when women, perhaps like Michael's girl-friend—let's call her Michelle—try to trick men into mar-riage, they're acting on the equally irrational belief in a happy marriage through sexual blackmail, and using that belief to justify their chicanery. If both are believing what they want to believe, they're equally playing dumb to what they don't. He wants to ignore that, short of sexual absti-nence, no birth control is guaranteed; while she wants to ignore that, feeling had, he might cut and run or stay and smoulder. And when the ignored-for-being-feared happens, each feels betrayed—which they have been, of course, but less by each other than their own self-delusions. For the gun that went off was all the time loaded, a discomforting fact they chose to ignore.

To his credit, Michael at least feels responsible for the child. In that, he distances himself from the millions of today's bug-out dads. Often seeing themselves as innocent victims of female wile or lapse, they cast the pregnancy as her problem, not theirs. She can decide to have the kid and raise it, or not. But whereas derelict males often can make their pseudo-innocence pay off by skipping out, the females they leave behind cannot. Like it or not, blameless or not, fair or not, it's they who ordinarily must decide whether to bear or abort, and then live with the choice.

More than thirty years ago, Margaret Sanger, the founder of Planned Parenthood who coined the phrase *birth control*, associated the liberation of women with reproductive choice. Sanger believed that no woman could call herself free until she owned or controlled her body—until she could choose consciously whether she would or would not be a mother.

Since its introduction in the United States in 1960, the pill certainly has given women Sanger's reproductive autonomy and made possible their full emancipation. But it hasn't overturned the time-honored tradition of assigning reproductive and child-rearing responsibilities primarily to women. Indeed, the pill has handed feckless fathers a potential trump. After all, prior to its development, no male could disown fatherhood by pleading the implicit ignorance of "But I thought you were on the pill!" nor could they accuse the woman of being either careless for forgetting to take the pill or treacherous for forgetting on purpose.

So, in counterpoint to its ordinary depiction as a quantum leap forward in the female struggle for freedom, the pill can also be viewed as an escalation through medical technology of the historic tendency to blame, distrust, and demonize women. Placed in that context, "But I thought you were on the pill!" can serve to maintain male power and false innocence, on one hand, and female oppression and undeserved guilt, on the other. As such it can represent an extension of—not a break with—age-old myths about women and men, their roles and relationships, both private and public. Of more than mere philosophical interest, these myths of gender help shape the male's and female's respective views of privilege and power, personal freedom and possibility, individual rights and self-responsibilities. So, caller Michael's is no mere hackneyed tale of what to do and who's to blame when the sexual gun goes off. It's an allegory of the transgenerational

influences that continue to help shape intersexual relations and relationships, and that neither Michael nor
Michelle—indeed, none of us—can ignore without risk
or rebuke.

What all the M&M's—Michaels and Michelles—should
know, and are responsible for *not* knowing, is that in the
West—not to mention other cultures—the woman as
scapegoat, and worse, is a familiar theme. It's evident in the
thought and teaching of the early Christian writers—
Tertullian, Ambrose, John Chrysostom, Augustine—and in
later ones—Thomas Aquinas, for instance. The M&M's and
the rest of us needn't be theologians or philosophers, but
we must be self-accountable for enough cultural awareness
to recognize that, by theologian and philosopher, woman
traditionally has been depicted variously as an Eve, sinner,
criminal, and seducer; as a necessary evil, inescapable punishment, and foe of friendship; as chaos and darkness, as
defective and misbegotten, as being created corporeally for
man and for reproduction. In Martin Luther's words (and
caller Michael's sentiments): It's women with their "tricks
and cunning" that deceive men.[3] Similarly, the M&M's don't
need to be feminists or social anthropologists, but they (and
we) should be—and are responsible for *not* being—self-
accountable enough to realize that the demonization of
women has been cross-cultural, and their degradation and
subjugation are by no means ancient history. (Even in the
modern era, for example, we hear voices of male "wisdom"
discrediting female capacities for anything but housekeep-
ing and childbearing—for anything but "the pleasure, joy
and solace of their husbands," to quote Luther's opinion,
which Pope Leo XIII shared and expressed in his famous

encyclical *Rerum Novarum* [1901].) What's more, the M&M's needn't be students of literature but they are accountable for being generally aware of the innumerable vicious put-downs of "uppity" females by the male intelligentsia, such as essayist Sam Johnson's likening a woman's preaching to "a dog's walking on his hind legs. It's not done well, but you are surprised to find it done at all."[4] Or like this catalog of female infirmities from the German philosopher Arthur Schopenhauer:

> It is only the man whose intellect is clouded by his sexual impulses that could give the name of *the fair sex* to that under-sized, narrow-shouldered, broad-hipped and short-legged race; for the whole beauty of the sex is bound up with this impulse. Instead of calling them beautiful, there would be more warrant for describing women as the unaesthetic sex. Neither for music nor for poetry, nor for fine art, have they really and truly any sense of susceptibility; it is a mere mockery if they make a pretense of it in order to assist their endeavor to please.[5]

In short, Michael and Michelle aren't required to be scholar or expert to know—to be accountable for knowing—something about the myths of gender that continue to shape relationships between the sexes. It simply won't do for them or us to burrow deeper into a cave of ignorance and continue to play dumb to the fact that, perhaps, the kindest face that can be put on the profile of woman that emerges across the generations and cultures is woman as either guardian or plaything of man—as either "drudges, or toys beneath man," the progressive Thomas Huxley lamented, "or a sort of angels above him."[6]

Happily for women, and for men, at least in First World countries, the worst abuses of the old male-master/female-slave paradigm are behind them. But even in the West, the vestiges of patriarchy and centuries-old sexism still can be seen in today's movies, merchandising, and MTV, where women continue to be depicted as objects of sex and violence. It can be felt in the low self-regard of too many girls and women (and the excessive self-esteem of too many boys and men) and in their preoccupation with appearance and pleasing. It resonates in Michael's bitter anger toward what he views as female cunning, and it comes through in Michelle's manipulation of sex, the one power sex objects always have had. It can be detected in the millions of women who choose to stay with abusive men, or rely on some man's passion and power to save them from drab, uneventful lives. It can be heard in the venomous rhetoric of radio brutes and bullies, and in the logic-chopping of political pooh-bahs and ecclesiastical troglodytes. It lurks in the statistics that report that one-third of all American children are born to unwed *mothers,* but say nothing of the unwed *fathers;* that the percentage of unwed mothers has nearly tripled in the last twenty-five years, but say nothing of unwed *fathers;* that in some states 70 percent of teen *mothers* are unmarried and that only 6 percent of teenage *mothers* get married, but again say nothing of the unmarried teenage *fathers.* It oozes out of so much we hear today of unwed and welfare mothers, and so little of their male counterparts. No wonder illegitimacy is framed largely as a female problem; no wonder too many males still earn their manhood by conquering, then absconding.

Honorably enough, though, Michael isn't ducking out of his parental responsibilities. His problem, he says, is that although he feels responsible for the child, he despises the child's mother. How can he do the right thing, he wants to know, when he has been so wronged?

"For the sake of the kid," Dr. Laura tells him, "you've got to learn to get along and be nice to each other." Then she reminds him, "You ought to be able to sit in a room and look at her if you were able to get naked and do it with her."[7] Indeed.

Perhaps, Michael will be one of the unmarried dads to do right by his child. Maybe he just needed the no-nonsense, straight-from-the-hip, tell-it-like-it-is advice Dr. Laura gave him in order to straighten up and fly right. Still, his feeling of being wronged nags—the bitter anger he feels toward the mother of his child worries. In the same breath that he says he feels responsible for the child, he almost disclaims the responsibility with: "*but* I don't know what to do because I'm so angry with her" (emphasis added). Will Michael (or will he not) keep the rage he feels from doing well what he must well do? Will he (or not) stop the bitterness from spilling out and poisoning his best efforts to be a good dad? We'll have to stay tuned, but one thing's for sure: To fully meet the new reality of fatherhood, Michael must come to grips with the full measure of his own complicity, which goes well beyond the biological fact that he fathered the child.

Does Michael realize, for example, that he set up Michelle as much as she did him? that he likely gave her good reason to believe that he cared for her more than he did—for believing that he was one of those men who, though tricked, do happily marry? Does he really see that he was trying to escape reproductive responsibility by placing the full burden of birth control on her? that he perhaps didn't even ask her how she felt about taking the pill; or about being told, "No children!"; or about sleeping with a man who, in effect, was saying "I love you—unless you get pregnant"? And most important, how will Michael now deal with the whole experience? Will he let it shape his relationships with other women—in and outside the bedroom—for the better or the bitter? Has he learned anything about his unfair and unreasonable attitudes, or will he continue to play dumb to them by only finding in the sordid affair corroboration of every gender stereotype he's ever unthinkingly absorbed? The choice is between Michael's remaining a child or becoming an adult.

And what of Michelle, the pregnant trickster? Perhaps she's learned something about self-deception. Perhaps she now sees how she was kidding herself about Michael, playing dumb to his true feelings. Perhaps she understands how she might have let her insecurities override her good sense, that if Michael valued her only for sex maybe it was because she presented herself to him as of little more value other than for sex. Perhaps she's learned not to listen to airhead pals who never learned "what a tangled web we weave, when first we practice to deceive."[8] And, perhaps, by learning all of this— that is, by fully owning and owning up to her part—she'll make a favorable future of an impropitious past. Or, on the other hand, perhaps she won't learn any of this, but in the end will cop only to making a strategic blunder in the ongoing war between the sexes. If she does, then she'll be plunging deeper into the age-old myth that women are—in all respects other than generation—essentially flawed, incapable, and inadequate. If she does, then she'll be undercutting the psychological basis of enlarged personal freedom and responsibility, namely, a sense of one's own power.

As a new century dawns, the Michaels and Michelles are facing, or need to face, new realities.

*For the Michelles:* All human beings, not just males, need power. This calls for a strength and independence that at times may imperil what you've learned to view as security and protection. This is a moral power close to the nerve of personal responsibility, and goes well beyond the reproductive power made possible by the pill. In part it's the power to cast off the romantic myth of being saved and awakened by noble knight and princely kiss. It's the power *and the responsibility* to change and define *yourself* rather than some Michael. It's the power *and the responsibility* to risk losing Michael by challenging his views about children and reproductive responsibility when he expresses them, not after the unwanted occurs. And if the unwanted does occur, it's the power *and the responsibility* to say and mean, "Michael, I accept my share of the blame, and I will hold you fully accountable for yours."

*For the Michaels:* All human beings, not only females, require some degree of emotional intimacy. This means a vulnerability and dependence you're not accustomed to. It also means the sharing of power and acceptance of new responsibilities. This is especially true in sexual conduct, where you can only meet your need for emotional intimacy by owning and owning up to your behavior, rather than disowning it with juvenile and patriarchal utterances like, "But I thought you were on the pill!"

———— • ◆ • ————

"However unjust and unreasonable the attitude we assume toward others, we seem to set in motion an automatic process which works blindly to corroborate and justify that attitude. It is an awesome thing that when we expose people, however undeservedly, to hatred, they tend to become hateful. Our prejudices, suspicion, and lies have this power to compel souls into a conforming pattern. It is as if the world, of its own accord, furnishes reasons for our unreasonable attitude."[9]

# 8. *"As a* (Whatever), *I Got a Right"*

I spent an educational afternoon recently with a long-time acquaintance. I learned a lot from "Will" about what passes for "rights" these days.

As Will and I browsed and shopped the local stores, I was impressed by the number of discounts available to "senior citizens," often taken to mean individuals sixty or older. But I was struck even more by how Will viewed these generational perks—not as courtesies or marketing ploys, but quasi-rights. He kept telling me that it was high time seniors like him were getting their "piece of the action," which he was grabbing with gusto. The hardware store, the nursery, the pharmacy—no establishment escaped Will's demand for preferential treatment now that he was well ensconced in the age of economic entitlement.

Lunch was no exception. Will got his senior discount; I was charged full price. At Will's request the waiter courteously filled up the bread basket several times, although neither of us consumed more than a slice or two. The remainder Will wrapped carefully in napkins and squirreled, together with a clutch of jam and butter packets, in his jacket for "later consumption." "Might as well take what we paid for," he said, and then chided me for hairsplitting when I suggested that we'd only paid for what we consumed on the premises. Changing the subject but not the message, he boasted about how he'd just carpeted his guest house with the money he'd made on a padded insurance claim for storm damage. The point, I gathered, was that because he'd paid a ton of homeowner premiums without ever before filing a claim, he was entitled to "exaggerate a little." "It's the American way," he laughed, as he began to calculate *his* share of the tab.

When we hit the streets, I was still trying to square Will's conduct and attitude with the other Will I knew—the one who says grace before meals and incessantly rails against the "unholy trinity," as he'd dubbed "crooked politicians," "slimy lawyers," and "welfare cheats."

"You ever feel funny about some of the stuff you do?" I asked him.

"Funny?" he said, his pockets bulging with booty. "Why should I feel funny? I've paid my dues. I'm only getting what I'm entitled to."

I asked him why he thought he was entitled to special consideration merely because he was a senior citizen. That's when he unloaded a fusillade about all the whiners and deadbeats getting something for nothing, like welfare recipients who buy booze and drugs with the hard-earned money of taxpayers like him.

"But aren't we all on welfare of one sort or another?" I asked him.

"Not me!" he protested. "I've never taken a dime of welfare in my whole life. And I'm damn proud of that."

I reminded him of the $23,000 government check he'd received the year before when warm weather killed his cherry crop.

"That's a farm subsidy," he said, "not welfare."

"What about the Social Security check you're taking every month even though you don't need it?"

"I paid for those benefits, every penny of it. I'm just getting back what's rightfully mine."

Reminding him that he'd long since recouped every penny he'd put into Social Security didn't impress Will. He said that if I doubted that he was entitled to collect as long as he lived, and his widow thereafter, he could produce reams of literature from the AARP (American Association of Retired Persons) to prove it. Not wanting to press the matter, I suggested a cup of coffee and a piece of pie instead.

"Good idea," he said. "I know just the place."

"I bet you do," I laughed, as we melted into the crowd.

Like many of us today, my friend Will is acutely conscious of a group he's a member of. He's a "senior citizen." I happen to be a "middle-aged white male." You may be a "disabled person," or "physically challenged" if you prefer, or "otherly abled." Someone else is a "single parent," "Native American," "recovering alcoholic," or "homeless person." Whatever we see ourselves as often makes us feel that we deserve special consideration or treatment.

The various rights movements of the past thirty-some-odd years haven't raised the consciousness of just select members of society, such as minorities and women. They've made virtually all of us more aware of the significant groups we belong to by birth, choice, or circumstance, and, like Will, we're hungry for our slice of the pie. Heightening this awareness, sharpening this appetite, is the plethora of ad hoc groups and organizations that have formed to spell out, support, and champion the perceived rights and interests of their victim-members. It's little wonder, then, that more and more, because we are this or that, we assert one right or another. Thus:

> "As a woman, I got a right . . ."
> "As a minority member, I got a right . . ."
> "As a single parent, I got a right . . ."
> "As a disabled person, I got a right . . ."
> "As a working person, I got a right . . ."
> "As a homeless person, I got a right . . ."
> "As a business person, I got a right . . ."
> "As a victim of child abuse, I got a right . . ."
> "As an adult child of an alcoholic parent, I got a right . . ."
> "As a prisoner, I got a right . . ."
> "As an economically disadvantaged (or gifted, or re-entry) student, I got a right . . ."
> "As a property owner, I got a right . . ."

And, of course, the granddaddy of all claims to rights based on group membership: "As a hard-working, God-fearing, taxpaying American, I got a right . . ."

As various groups strive for what they perceive as justice—usually defined economically—we increasingly identify with our groups. The upshot of this quickening "us-firstism" is that society increasingly fractures into competing interest groups: nonwhite vs. white, women vs. men, liberal vs. conservative, pro-life vs. pro-choice, the younger generation vs. the older, cities vs. counties, states vs. Washington. But why stop there? Cyclists vs. motorists, fat vs. thin, left-handed vs. right-handed, bald vs. hirsute—the opposition possibilities would dazzle the imagination if they weren't so real. In such a divisive social environment, the responsibility-forged ties that bind threaten to snap, leaving the republic for which the flag stands: many nations, divisible, with justice for me and mine. How long can the center hold in a society where the many shout, "I got a right!" while only the few will admit, "I got a responsibility"?

If the obsession with group power and privilege has made ours a house divided, it has rendered its occupants largely indifferent to one another. In becoming supersensitive to the relations of human communities, we tend to overlook the relations of individuals within those communities, to see individuals less as persons than as representatives of particular groups, which we may or may not like. What we owe one another as human beings can, thus, get lost in the calculus of group rights and interests.

Lost, too, is the fact that rights entail responsibilities, the most basic of which is determining whether or not to exercise a right. What we're entitled to do may not be what we ought to do; what's permissible may not be proper. What we actually ought to do—what our responsibility as opposed to our right is—calls for a careful weighing and weighting of the legitimate rights and interests of other parties, which in turn requires, among other virtues, considerable self-discipline. It also requires that a sharp line be drawn between the moral and social behavior of individuals and of social groups, lest individual conscience be sacrificed to political strategy. But such important distinctions—as between what we may and what we should do, and between individual and group morality—can get blurred in the group's unrestrained pursuit of power and privilege. Also obscured: the individual selfishness that often operates under the rubric of group rights.

Take the person who ordinarily would never deliberately endanger her neighbor. She might do just that, however, in zealous pursuit of what she thinks she's entitled to as a "property owner" or "businessperson." Thus the owner of a plumbing supply store who sued for the right to pave an entire parking lot, regardless of the fact that it was in a floodplain and that leaving just 10 percent of the lot free would reduce the downstream flooding risk to other property owners and businesspersons. The city had to compensate the woman to leave a sliver of her lot unpaved.[1] In other words, she had to be paid to do the responsible thing.

Sometimes it may even be our own families who must pay the freight for our personally self-serving exercise of a group's right. Will, for example, reflexively opposes any entitlement reform that threatens the status quo of Social Security and Medicare. As a "senior citizen" he feels entitled to a full measure of both, regardless of his affluence. Okay, but what of his grandchildren, and the tens of millions of other grandchildren? Is he also entitled to mortgage their future? Looking through the lens of the group, he sees the collective right but not the individual responsibility. He sees what he's entitled to but plays dumb to what others are entitled to.

About fifty years ago the theologian and moralist Reinhold Niebuhr drew a sharp distinction between the moral and social behavior of individuals and groups. Individuals may be moral, he said, in the sense that they can

act altruistically. But human societies and social groups cannot, or at least not as easily. "In every group," Niebuhr wrote
in *Moral Man and Immoral Society,* "there is less reason to guide
and to check impulse, less capacity for self-transcendence,
less ability to comprehend the needs of others and therefore
more unrestrained egoism than the individuals, who com-
pose the group, reveal in their personal relationships."[2]

As a consequence of their inherent "moral obtuseness,"
their lack of moral imagination and sympathy, Niebuhr
regarded the selfishness of human communities as
inevitable—and escalating. The more extreme the selfishness of one group, the more extreme the reactions of others. Moral and rational persuasion—the glue of civilized
society—ultimately breaks down. Only coercion and force
can deter competing interest groups as they press for more
and more.

Today, as we rally behind the banners of our preferred
groups and dispatch our lobbyists to seats of governance, it's
worth keeping in mind that our collective behavior isn't
always amenable to reason or conscience. We might ponder
the place of individual conscience within the conscienceless
collective. Do mature, responsible adults merely accede to
the always self-serving and often brutal character built into
the behavior of all groups? May the individual members
operate without reason and sensibility as their interest
groups are naturally inclined to? May they stop thinking for
themselves and simply go along?

Niebuhr thought not. "The needs of an adequate political
strategy," he wrote, "do not obviate the necessity for culti-
vating the strictest individual moral discipline and the most
uncompromising idealism."[3] In other words, what's politi-

cally right may not be morally right. What's good for a particular group may not be good for society as a whole. Individuals cannot use group loyalty to play dumb to the opportunity and responsibility they always have to the highest canons of personal morality. This means always measuring the group against one's highest ideals; and when groups lapse, it means challenging, even quitting them. (Perhaps former president Bush so acted when he resigned his longstanding membership in the National Rifle Association when the NRA equated federal agents with Nazi storm troopers in a fund-raising letter.) Most important, doing the morally right—as opposed to the politically correct thing—also means never losing sight of individual character, of the virtues we can and must cultivate to remain mature, responsible adults in the sociocentric environment. Virtues such as:

*individual moral discipline*—no matter the group we belong to, individual moral discipline is always required and possible;

*self-restraint*—no matter the importance of the particular group's mission, self-restraint is always required and possible;

*goodwill and cooperation*—no matter the nobility of the group's struggle, or its struggle for nobility, goodwill and cooperation are always required and possible.

———— • ◆ • ————

As political beings, we can always find good reason to cluck, "I got a right." But it takes a mature moral being to stop and ask: "But do I have an overriding responsibility?"

# 9. *"It's Legal, Isn't It?"*

Sometimes I pose the following situation to my business ethics class:

Imagine you own a small garment company that sells fire-retardant children's pajamas. Orders are pouring in by the thousands when suddenly you're informed by the U.S. Consumer Protection and Safety Commission that you must stop selling the sleepwear because their fire-retardant chemical has been found to cause kidney cancer in children. You are instructed to dispose of the dangerous PJs by burying or burning, or using them as industrial wipe cloths. Either way, of course, you stand to lose thousands of dollars. Then, just when it appears you will have to eat the losses, you are contacted by an exporter who is willing to pay you 10 to 30 percent on the wholesale dollar for the opportunity to dump the carcinogenic PJs overseas, specifically in Third World countries.[1]

*Question: What is the first thing you'd think about?*

The answer I most often get is: "Is it legal?" I inform the class that the ban applies only to domestic, not foreign sales. Then I ask them what they'd do: take the loss or sell the pajamas? A large number would try to recoup their losses, even if it meant endangering the health of children abroad. The case they make most is summed up in the rhetorical question: "It's legal, isn't it?"

I suspect that these students aren't unique or even unusual. The law is the first and sometimes the last thing that many of us think about in defining our relations and responsibilities to one another. We play dumb to most other concerns, most notably the moral ones. That's largely why we have so many laws, for laws multiply when self-discipline and self-responsibility break down—when too many individuals are more concerned with what's legal than what's right, with what they can get away with than what they ought to do.

Laws are intended to institutionalize the highest moral ideals of a people. Were we always true to those ideals, we'd need no laws—we'd be self-regulating. That we have legal limits in almost every area of our lives is public proof of countless individual failures to honor some ideal or other, which law piled upon law can do little to alter. The more numerous its laws, the more corrupt the society.

With the proliferation of laws have come countless lawsuits. Nowadays you can sue or be sued for just about anything. True, the outcome is never certain, but more and more the greed of winning and fear of losing drive the conduct of individuals, institutions, and professions.

A highly litigious society like ours both reflects and reinforces a mystified, perfectionistic notion of what human beings and human relations are. It leaves little room for lapses and errors, even honest ones. It makes the unexpected, the unforeseen, and the unintentional the mother lode of greedy plaintiffs and hungry lawyers. Presto! Accidents turn into torts. Abracadabra! Before our disbelieving eyes, simple wear and tear, ordinary aches and pains, normal stress and anxiety, all magically become compensation claims. Clap your hands and acts of God turn into failures of man. No mistaking it, in the ligitious society, "To err is liable, to forgive bovine."

Of course, the world of tort law is no harmlessly entertaining magic show. A minefield is more like it, which the prudent avoid or tread cautiously. And so physicians insure to the teeth and practice "defensive medicine," thereby ratcheting up the cost of health care. Small business owners incorporate, hoping to create a protective shield against being personally destroyed. Homeowners scurry to protect themselves against the most bizarre of liabilities, like an injury sustained by a thief while burglarizing their home.

I recall once being urged to take out an "umbrella" policy. This, I was informed, would shelter me against any conceivable legal storm. Perplexed, I asked the zealous agent for an example of an injury I might cause person or property that ordinary liability wouldn't cover. He thought for a while before saying, "Well, suppose you run into someone in the supermarket with your shopping cart." He paused to make sure I took the bait. Then he beamed, "If they sued, you'd be covered." Gotcha! I imagined crippling someone in a mad dash from produce to dairy. Could I ever shop again without the security of the umbrella? Not likely. It was either spring for the additional coverage or shop with a handcart. Needless to say I sprang. Now I can drive with reckless abandon up and down the aisles of any supermarket—in North America, at least.

Beyond "simple" tort many other legal pitfalls await today's unwary. Even in the post–affirmative action era wise employers had better consider the sex, complexion, last names, and physical and emotional health of job applicants as much as their qualifications, lest they invite unfair discrimination suits. Police had better watch how much force they use on lawbreakers, lest they violate their civil liberties. Workers and supervisors had better be careful about how they address one another, lest they trigger a sexual harassment suit. And parents had better think twice before swatting their unruly child on the tush; they could be sued for child abuse, and even lose the child. No doubt about it, "The United States," as Chief Justice Hughes once observed, "is the greatest law factory the world has ever known"—and that was sixty years ago!

It's tempting and dishonest to ascribe the explosion of laws and suits only to sophistic lawyers, addle-headed judges, and cockeyed juries. They're key players, to be sure. Too often the courtroom does prove exactly what H. L. Mencken said it was: "A place where Jesus Christ and Judas Iscariot would be equals, with the betting odds in favor of Judas."[2] But too many of us, by our careless, mean-spirited, or wanton behavior help make ours a lawsuit-looney landscape:

- the industrialist whose "efficient operation" includes midnight dumping of toxic waste in a vacant lot
- the advertiser who misleads or manipulates
- the businessperson who will do anything for a buck
- the cigarette smoker who sees a constitutional right to light up wherever she chooses
- the gun owner who can't distinguish between hunting and assault weapons

- the teenager who won't turn down the boom box while cruising Main Street
- the motorist who uses the highway as a trash can
- the seniors whose medications and sundry infirmities make them road menaces
- the dog walker who won't clean up after his pet
- the worker who imports his racial and sexual stereotypes, biases, and hatreds into the workplace
- the God-fearing who disrupt and destroy with their fanaticism
- the athletic coaches who by example teach the kids that winning is everything—that nice guys finish last—and the parents and boosters who go along with it
- all of us who have forgotten that human beings are fallible, and that accidents really do happen

Blame "the system" if you like, but the truth is that we are as much to blame for the explosion of laws and suits as those who directly profit from them.

If we were more caring and considerate, more respectful and fair-minded, more understanding and empathetic, we'd have fewer laws because we'd need laws less. Edmund Burke nailed it two centuries ago when he said that manners mean more than laws. "Upon them," said the political philosopher, "in a great measure, the laws depend." He explained as follows:

The law touches us but here and there, and now and then. Manners are what vex or smooth, corrupt or purify, exalt or debase, barbarize or refine us, by a constant, steady, uniform, insensible operation, like that of the air we breathe in. They give their whole form and color to our lives. According to their quality, they aid morals, they supply them, or they totally destroy them.[3]

If the legal opinion is the one we mainly seek and heed today; if we ignore the philosopher, humor the sociologist, dismiss the psychologist, and devalue the artist; if TV has created the celebrity lawyer and classrooms full of wannabes; if coverage of "O.J."—in and out of the courtroom—was mainly hour after hour after pettifogging hour of lawyering, there's good reason. In the litigious society, the lawyer is king.

One would think that our contemporary obsession with law—with what we can get away with and can't, with what we can sue and be sued for—would make us more personally responsible. Just the opposite: The more legalistically we frame it, the narrower our spectrum of self-responsibility. We start to equate legality with morality, such that the legal becomes the moral, and the moral becomes whatever isn't legal. "Is it legal?" replaces "Is it moral?" as the locus of moral deliberation. As the limits of the law come to mark the limits of individual responsibility, the "moral" person becomes a cost accountant. And permeating the social atmosphere like a coiling miasma are considerations of "upside" and "downside," loopholes and fine print, game plans and one-upmanship, calculated risks and number crunching. Morality becomes casuistry.

———— ◆ ————

"Law," Thoreau said, "never made men a whit more just."[4] But it might make us less just—and less honest, truthful, caring, and kind to boot. For where law is the sole determinant of right and wrong, right and wrong cease to determine conduct. When "It's legal, isn't it?" is the best we can say in our defense, we've lost our sense of the best we can do.

# 10. *"Don't Sweat the Small Stuff"*

Iknew I was in trouble when I spotted "Don't Sweat the Small Stuff" on a door marked EMPLOYEES ONLY in the auto repair shop. Actually, the complete sign read: TWO RULES TO LIVE BY: (1) DON'T SWEAT THE SMALL STUFF. (2) EVERYTHING IS SMALL STUFF. I suppose the inference that one shouldn't sweat anything was intended to be amusing. It scared me. Frankly, the thought of placing my car in the hands of a graduate of the "Don't sweat anything" school of auto mechanics is about as comforting as being told by the pilot of a plane with Bart Simpson painted on its nose, "We don't ever want to be accused of taking ourselves too seriously."

That same day I read a newspaper article about widespread petty theft. In it an attorney admitted he'd wait for someone to buy a newspaper from a sidewalk rack and grab the door before it shut in order to get his paper free. He also had perfected the art of jarring a parking meter just right so that it registers time on it. He could afford the newspaper and parking, so why did he do it? "You figure the newspaper company makes so much money," he explained, "taking one paper won't matter."[1]

A quarter for a newspaper or for parking—such a small thing, why sweat it? Or soda pop, for that matter. In the same article a telemarketer confessed going into certain food chains, ordering a sandwich, and then asking for a free cup to get some water. He'd then use the cup to drink "as much pop as I can handle."

Idle awhile at the salad bar of a modern supermarket and you're bound to spot a grazer or two. Evidently, for some of us, a cantaloupe chunk or carrot stick is so trivial that popping a piece or two isn't really stealing. Sometimes the kids join in at the invitation of Mom or Dad, who probably doesn't realize that they're feeding the tykes more than a piece of fruit. They're teaching them not to sweat the small stuff, and not teaching them the difference between what's theirs and what's not.

On one occasion I witnessed a row between a shopper and a produce manager. It seems that while Mother was carefully selecting grapes, Junior was popping them. The produce person gently informed the child, who was about seven, that the grapes were for sale, not sampling, whereupon Mom sprang to her child's defense. "Oh, for heaven's sake!" she said indignantly. "It's such a small thing."

I wondered exactly where she'd draw the line between a "small" thing and a "big" thing. Perhaps at the point of peeling or opening, as with bananas and oranges, or soft drinks and milk. The only distinction the child seemed capable of making was between what he wanted and what he didn't. And he wanted those grapes. Whether Mom corrected Junior in private we'll never know. But her public message to him and anyone within hearing was clear and direct: "Don't sweat the small stuff." In other words, stealing "small stuff" is okay; indeed, it's not really stealing at all.

Certainly "Don't sweat the small stuff" can be sage advice when taken to mean something like "Keep cool," "Maintain your perspective," or "Avoid overreacting." But care is called for. Individuals who have contempt for the small stuff ordinarily have contempt for people and property. Employed thoughtlessly, not sweating the small stuff ceases to function as a guideline for rational living and becomes a rationale for living without guidelines. It's then—when we want the newspaper or parking free, or the hotel's towels, hangers, and lightbulbs, or the office stationery and stamps; when we want ten minutes more on the treadmill than the club's rules permit while others are waiting; when we want to help ourselves to a handful of trail mix and swill the soft drinks—it's then that we're most likely to minimize the object of our desire. "It's such a small thing that taking it really doesn't matter," we can persuade ourselves, regardless that what we want belongs or matters to someone else. Treating what we covet as trivial allows us to ignore the inconvenient fact of ownership and provides us a convenient alibi to pilfer with impunity.

One day in my business ethics class a young woman raised a provocative question about company-owned property. She had recently left a job, and upon leaving had helped herself to copies of the company's client data, which she intended to draw upon in starting up her own business. She wanted to know if she'd done anything wrong.

The ensuing discussion centered mainly on whether or not she intended to compete with her former employer. Because she didn't, few objected to her conduct. "After all," went the consensual logic, "she's not hurting anyone." Or, as one basketball fan put it, "No harm, no foul."

But not everyone was convinced. A handful insisted that the client data was the company's property and, therefore, she had no right to utilize it without their permission. To this argument the student replied, "But I didn't think the company would mind. I mean, it was no big deal—just a bunch of names and numbers."

"Then why didn't you ask first?" someone wanted to know.

The student smiled before sheepishly saying, "They might've said no"—allowance that she'd kept herself dumb by not asking permission.

In the proverbial "grand scheme of things," soft drinks, newspapers, parking meters, and client lists don't add up to a hill of beans in a salad bar. But neither does a horseshoe nail; and yet for the want of one a kingdom was lost. "A little neglect will breed great mischief," Ben Franklin warned.[2] The kingdom lost may be a marriage, friendship, or career.

---

In human relations one can easily suffer lapses, even stupid ones. The forgetful spouse, the scatterbrained friend, the slow worker, the preoccupied motorist, the harried shopper, the overworked clerk—these are stock players, major and minor, in the dramas of our lives. But once forfeited, trust can't be regained. "He bought a lamp for a very high price," said Epictetus of the man who stole his lantern. "For a lamp he became a thief, for a lamp he became faithless, for a lamp he became beast-like."[3] Two millennia later the judgment of the Stoic philosopher resounds with reproof to those whose honor is worth no more to them than the price of some "small stuff."

# 11. *"Look Out for Number 1"*

So jealous of his recipes is he that the pastry chef says he won't share them with his own brother. At seventy, he's as excited as he was at fourteen, when he appropriated the recipes from the bakery he worked in as a kid. "Whatever recipes I could steal, I'd write down," he says. Then, referring to the custard tarts he's decorating, he proudly declares, "This recipe goes back to 1939 . . . and it's still the same." The newspaper article profiling the pastry chef sums up his life as "a recipe for pursuit of perfection."[1]

Is there anything wrong with this picture? Probably not by conventional standards. The baker, after all, saw an opportunity and seized it. True, the opportunity was, by his own account, theft. But he didn't get caught, and he made it work. What could be more American?

Many of us today are like the baker. Self-absorbed, we seek personal advantage at work and play, even at home, often with disregard to the costs. Little wonder that incidents of cheating, deception, and discourtesy—"small stuff"—are on the rise. We "fudge" on our taxes, pad our résumés, shave a couple of years off our age. We cheat—on tests, insurance claims, and spouses, in business and sport.

Athletes sometimes enhance performance with drugs, or try to sabotage an opponent; even scientists have been known to massage their research findings. On the highways, far too many of us speed, tailgate, run lights, cut off, and recklessly lane-change, all to gain an edge. If called to account on our incivility, we're more likely to snap, sneer, or stonewall than simply to say: "I'm sorry, how thoughtless of me." We play dumb rather than own up.

Few activities, relationships, occupations, or institutions, it seems, are spared the exploits of those looking out strictly for Number 1. And sometimes it pays off. More than occasionally the classroom cheater gets an A, the slumlord gets rich, and the unsavory politician gets elected. Doubtless, too, many a liar has avoided the blame and shame visited on the truth teller; and Good Samaritans, sad to say, have been sued by those they unselfishly attempted to assist. In short, blind as it is, justice doesn't always happen to people; and— as the baker proves—by the competitive coin of the realm, honesty is not always the best policy.

But let's not ignore the flip side: the costs of looking out strictly for Number 1. The authors of one book on business ethics point out that ethical naïveté ends careers "more quickly and more definitively than any other mistake in judgment and accounting."[2] They say that acts of lying, cheating, stealing, or double-dealing are neither easily forgiven nor soon forgotten, in or outside business. "For every case of known unethical conduct that goes unpunished, a dozen once-promising careers silently hit a dead-end or quietly go down the tubes." And the saddest part of all is that sometimes the cheaters or liars may keep their jobs and never realize they've been found out. Their careers just go nowhere.[3] Poetically enough, then, those looking out strictly for Number 1 can end up not first but last.

How is it that we can fail, at times miserably, to serve ourselves while attempting to serve no one but ourselves? How to explain this boomerang effect?

Sometimes we never calculate the costs: The blind ambition of the careerist sees no risk, only reward. Other times we're not fully aware of what we're doing: Drenched in a competitive ethic where the dog that snaps the quickest gets the bone, we try to get away with what we can. Beyond this, our best-laid, self-serving plans often go awry because we hold a narrow, inadequate, and even false sense of our own best interests. We sell ourselves short. We confuse our real needs with desires for money, power, and ego satisfaction. Ignored and unfed are our moral and spiritual needs. Were these included in its general understanding, "Look out for Number 1" might be a practical principle of self-love. But as ordinarily practiced, this self-interest principle is not self-love. Neither is it a friend of personal responsibility nor a formula for success.

In fact, "Look out for Number 1" represents and fosters a shallow view of self and others as no more and no less than materially acquisitive beings. By urging us to prefer ourselves first, last, and always, "me-firstism" insures what Henri Amiel called "the survival of the animal in us"—self-interest. Lost is our humanity, which the Swiss philosopher said "begins . . . with self-surrender."[4] As a maxim for the unmoderated pursuit of self-interest, "Look out for Number 1" substitutes having for being, while making a virtue of selfishness and an imperative of self-gratification. Erecting its center in itself, it lacks in social interest, which for psychologist Alfred Adler was at the root of all personal failures.[5] Where there's no social interest, there's no basis for community or personal responsibility, and little in the way of an ideal to which individual or society can aspire.

As a philosophy of life, "Look out for Number 1" lacks in social interest but not in social affiliation; for what we can't get working on our own, we'll often seek to acquire through collective action. We join up with others who want what we want for ourselves. Thus today, perhaps more than ever before, individuals of like fears and interests are uniting for a self-aggrandizement that may or may not parallel the social good.

But there's more involved in collective action than self-enrichment, more than the insistence on this protection or that right as a member of one interest group or another. Of greater significance for self-responsibility is the powerful bond that can form between individual and group—so strong a bond that members can come to perceive that group's fate as their own. Personal interests can become indistinguishable from group interests, even cease to exist outside the shape and form given them by the collective mind. Individual thought can give way to "groupthink," and the inner voice of personal conscience can be drowned out by the outer roar of authority. When this happens, then "Look out for Number 1" becomes identical with "Look out for ourselves." Then the personal advantage seeker becomes the "true believer," who always and unthinkingly seeks the group's social advantage. With the successful transformation of "me-firstism" into "us-firstism," the last sliver of social interest disappears, the final murmurings of individual conscience fade out, and the faintest gleamings of self-responsibility flicker and die. There remains only the collective mind, with its conceptual and rhetorical convolutions, and the collective will to carry them out. "When the flag is unfurled," reminds the saying, "all reason is in the trumpet."

In his book *Where Do We Go From Here: Chaos or Commitment?* Martin Luther King Jr. wrote: "It seems to be a fact of life that human beings cannot continue to do wrong without eventually reaching out for some rationalization to clothe their acts in the garments of righteousness."[6] King had slavery in mind when he wrote these words in 1967—specifically, how white supremacists used the Bible and religion to support their belief in the basic superiority of the white race. If theology could be used to give slavery a moral veneer, why not logic? Thus, the following "argument" formulated for the inferiority of the "Negro":

> All men are made in the image of God;
> God, as everybody knows, is not a Negro:
> Therefore the Negro is not a man.[7]

King's point about how we can make God a partner and logic a weapon in our ugliest of perversions stands as a general warning about the human capacity to rationalize virtually anything. As Professor Richard Paul, internationally recognized expert on teaching critical thinking, has observed: Groups looking out strictly for themselves exhibit on a massive scale the same sort of twisted logic and self-serving rationalization to justify their behavior as individual egoists do.[8] Thus, for the group as much as for the individual, selfish desire can pose as self-preservation. So, too, blind justice can pose as noble principle, oppression as care, and control as love. Callous disregard can masquerade as genuine concern, expediency as fairness; belief as fact, passion as sincerity, and sincerity as truth. If we're fully capable of such distortion to rationalize racism and even genocide, then how much easier to bridge what are logically unbridgeable gaps between what we say and do every day— even to the point of coating our self-serving actions with a patina of social responsibility. Thus:

- the pro-lifer who kills because life is so sacred
- the environmentalist who booby-traps the forest for the good of God's furry, little, tree-dwelling creatures
- the early-to-rise, often-to-ring proselytizer who "loves" you so much that she won't take "no soliciting" for "not interested" and "not interested" for an answer
- the demagogues, on the stump or on the air, who so want a more perfect union that they spoon-feed us a steady diet of hate and suspicion, of half-truths and whole cloth
- the righteous legislators who are so concerned with "family values" that they aim their budget-cutting weapons at the hungry and the handicapped, at programs for drug abuse and summer jobs for needy youth
- the religionists who breast-beat about world poverty but do nothing to help control population growth in the poorest nations of the world

If me-firsters lack in social interest, us-firsters do so with a vengeance. More than ignoring, trivializing, or playing dumb to the legitimate interests of other groups, they frame

them as implacable foes. In the extreme, the group's paranoia creates a siege mentality that casts the most modest
consideration to the other side as an act of betrayal or sub-
version, even suicide. Its individual members can come to
so identify their personal survival with the group's that they
interpret the slightest concession to "them," the enemy, as
the first step down a slippery slope that ultimately will end
with "them" getting everything: jobs, neighborhoods,
power, even countries and cultures. Contemporary history
bleeds with examples of this sort of rabid sociocentrism.
Witness the tribal wars in the Balkans, the Middle East,
Northern Ireland, the former Soviet republics, Central
Africa. Who but the "true believers" themselves can discern
interests different enough to warrant all the savagery?

If me-firsters are vulnerable to the boomerang effect, so
are us-firsters. Granted, group comeuppance sometimes is
long delayed. But eventually the boomerang returns, often to
strike relatively innocent group members. Who, for example, are today's self-declared victims of "reverse discrimination" but the white sons and grandsons of yesterday's bigots
and supremacists, who zealously insured for themselves the
inside lane in the race for power, privilege, and property? By
the same token, some of today's ethnic community leaders
don't realize the boomerang they hurl when they racialize
any effort to control ethnic gangs. Rather than roundly con-
demning wanton lawbreaking, no matter its source, they find
only another opportunity to hector about racist police and
civil liberty violations. They never realize that by so doing
they may be inadvertently condoning sociopathy and perpet-
uating a cycle of violence that, ironically, sustains the basis for
the very outlaw stereotyping they rail against. What gang

tough or wannabe, after all, is likely to soften when legitimated by a respected community leader or niggling legist?

Another potentially dangerous irony of us-firstism: the confusion, fear, and suspicion it can produce in its practitioners, who can end up distrusting and despising anyone who merely resembles its perceived enemy—even a potential friend and ally. Thus a Muslim can end up hating *any* Christian, a born-again fundamentalist *any* "unregenerate" one, a black person *any* white person, a woman *any* man, a pro-lifer *any* pro-choicer, a gun protector *any* gun controller—and vice versa. Today, it's reported, some gays who are HIV-negative are being rejected by some gays who are HIV-positive, who in turn are being rejected by the negatives for fear of getting AIDS. This despite the fact that gays who are free of HIV shoulder many of the same burdens as the infected gays do, especially homophobia. Not surprising. When superficial characteristics, facile labels, or single issues become the litmus tests of sincerity, sympathy, and goodwill, there's no basis for distinguishing friend from foe. Paranoia takes hold, and violence escalates.

How to maintain a sense of propriety, of moral independence and self-responsibility within the group? It takes courage to speak frankly to and about the groups we're members of—from our families to our nation. It takes character and conviction to confront the relative, colleague, or fellow club member who's the racist, sexist, or hate-monger. It takes a strong social interest to challenge our organizations when we're convinced they're out of line. Not only do we risk our position in the group, we test its credibility and integrity, perhaps even endanger its survival. But precisely because it takes pluck and because few can endure criticism gratefully and gracefully, where we venture to criticize our groups we're performing a remarkable act of responsibility, respect, and loyalty. "To undertake to wound or offend a man for his own good," said Montaigne, "is to have a healthy love for him."[9]

———— • ◆ • ————

Centered in itself, lacking in communitarianism, "Look out for Number 1" is a most dangerous form of dualistic thinking. It's exactly the "me vs. you," "us vs. them" mentality that keeps individuals dumb to the regard they owe themselves and others. On the individual level, "Look out for Number 1" gives license to cheat and steal. On the collective level it helps maintain all forms of oppression and domination, and breeds resentment, distrust, and often violence. In a society and world like ours—one of diverse and often colliding concerns—it's on the common ground, not the battleground, that we most responsibly serve our individual best interests.

# 12. *"Charity Begins at Home"*

This popular expression can be read as a lesson in ordering priorities when dispensing individual resources. "Charity begins at home" basically teaches that first and foremost we're responsible for setting our own house in order before helping others with theirs.

Why anyone would need to be reminded of homefront charity is puzzling. After all, we're naturally inclined to favor ourselves and look out for our own. And yet, "perplexed" like Keats "in a world of doubts and fancies,"[1] we can easily lose touch with this healthy instinct. Like many an ancient mariner, we can believe our path is straight and true when, in fact, it's wildly off course. The immoderate community activist comes to mind. A familiar type, this person is too busy doing good for others to be home in the afternoons when the kids get in from school, or help them with their homework, or teach them what it means to be a good older brother or sister to a younger one. The $2,000 computer in the family room is for all of that. But errant others are equally evident:

- the celebrity dubbed "role model" for his well-publicized charity work, which obscures the fact that he periodically uses his wife as a punching bag;

- the national politician too consumed with solving the nation's drug problems to notice that one of his own kids has a serious drinking problem;
- the devout churchgoer who gives till it hurts—and is encouraged to—no matter her own family's desperate state;
- the affluent parent whose confused notion of being a "good provider" substitutes late-model cars and generous credit cards for old-fashioned love and discipline;
- the workaholic with a street-of-dreams home and baubles to match, who is too pooped to pop when he gets home from work in the evening. A drink and some idle chatter is about all he can muster before dozing off. On weekends he unwinds with a round or two of golf or simple idling before the latest "big game" telecast. Monday morning finds his engine revving up for another seventy-hour work week. But it's all worth it, he assures himself and the world. After all, he can afford to send the kids to the best colleges in the country. Why, he can even afford to send them to the best therapists in town, although he'd rather that be kept secret.

It's safe but inaccurate to think that the millions of young children at risk in America today are born into poverty. Many are, of course. But the realities of modern life— parents who work long hours outside the home, single-parent families, substandard day care, the decline of the nuclear family, and the virtual disappearance of the extended one— can deprive children of middle- and upper-income families of the loving support they need during the critical early years of their lives. That's why central to any effort to reduce the hazards of growing up in modern America is a renewed and enlightened sense of parental responsibilities that interprets "Charity begins at home" as protecting, nurturing, and stimulating our children. They deserve no less, and *we owe them no more.*

The italicized portion of the last sentence is crucial to a mature understanding of "Charity begins at home." It implies that there's a limit to the charity that begins at home, beyond which we can harm, not help, our children and betray our parental responsibilities. Being mindful of this limit, which admittedly is vague and idiosyncratic but nonetheless important to set and enforce, guards against the inclination to rationalize overindulgence of children as home-front charity. In defining and adhering to a fair and reasonable limit, we gently but firmly guide our children in the direction of self-reliance, self-discovery, and self-acceptance. We also insure that the charity that begins at home doesn't end there. For, as the old saying goes, it takes a village to raise a child, which is to say: There are other children who need our help and protection. And there are other demands on our charity that extend beyond the home front that we shouldn't play dumb to.

Just before Christmas 1994, newspapers carried the account of a Little Rock businessman who was ordered to turn off most of the three million lights of the Christmas display on his mansion and the two homes he'd bought next door. The display, said the court, was a nuisance and safety hazard. Eight years earlier the man had first started stringing Christmas lights outside his home. Sometime between 1986 and 1994, the display had turned from a show into a spectacle of crosses, reindeer, angels, doors with lights, and six-foot-tall letters saying MERRY CHRISTMAS and HAPPY NEW YEAR. Atop a 120-foot-tall lighted cone on his roof spun a giant, luminous globe. Angels flew fifty feet in the air. Airline pilots reported seeing the display ten miles out.[2]

By the early 1990s thousands of cars a night would jam nearby streets, stopping traffic and blocking some neighbors from reaching their homes and sealing others in them. An elderly widow said her yard had been turned into a rubbish dump and latrine by the crowds who used it as a shortcut and sometimes turned belligerent when confronted. The man answered neighbors' complaints by expanding the display. Even a district court order to limit it to fifteen nights and end public tours didn't stop the expansion. It ultimately took an order from the Arkansas Supreme Court to force an end to the annual yuletide extravaganza. But the affair didn't end there. The businessman appealed to the U.S. Supreme Court, claiming freedom of religion and speech. The Court let the Arkansas ruling stand.

Why the Vegas-like light show? Why such annoying tintinnabulation? The businessman explained that it was all to please Breezy, his teenage daughter, who just loves Christmas. With tears in his eyes, he was quoted as saying, "I'd walk through fire to help a stranger. Imagine what I'd do for my family."[3]

Walking through fire for a stranger is an admirable moral sentiment, but *The Book of Common Prayer* teaches that "all our doings without charity are nothing worth."[4] Do we teach our children neighborly concern by indulging them at the neighbors' expense? Do we teach them to honor the rights of others by showing them how to disregard those rights? Do we teach them to respect money by showing them how to blow it on tons of tinsel and frivolous lawsuits? Do we teach them that with power and privilege come additional responsibilities of self-control and consideration by showing them how to use power and privilege arrogantly? In short, do we really expect them to learn the meaning of charity from our uncharitable example? Talk is never so cheap as when preaching virtue, and never so costly as when unhinged from action.

The greatest of home-front charities is teaching through living, not lecturing. No amount of parental pontificating about the value of school will convince the child whose parents don't care enough to attend parents' night. Very few teens will not experiment with sex whose single parents are themselves acting like teenagers. Not many youngsters are going to avoid alcohol and drugs if the company they keep isn't parentally policed. And very few of them will learn to like themselves for what they are, not for what they're expected to be, when the ball game is for winning, not enjoying; for competing, not cooperating; for besting and beating, not learning and fun. Forget all the religiosity and professions of faith, all the Sunday morning sermons and legally mandated Monday morning school prayers—none of it will help our kids if we're using worship to salve our own consciences rather than challenge our lifestyles. None of it will save them when more than 90 percent of us say that both selfishness and the condition of the poor are serious social problems, and nearly as many *also* say that having a beautiful home, a new car, and other nice things are very important to us. Our homes can shine with casino candlepower and jingle with jackpot jubilation, but they won't warm the hearts and

feed the souls of our children when religious values influence the job choice of only 10 percent of us, while money
does the rest.[5]

So we do need to keep our priorities straight in dispensing our limited, individual resources. The *genuine* needs and
interests of families must always come first. Philanthropists
who ignore the needs of their families are the worst kind of
misers. But while we're helping ourselves, let's play fair.
"Charity begins at home," said Dickens, "and justice begins
next door."[6]

———————•◆•———————

Charity does begin at home, but anyone governed by this
doctrine probably isn't charitable.

# 13. *"I Was Just Following Orders"*

The "over-the-hill gang" they've been called—that improbable collection of less than five hundred middle-aged men of Reserve Police Battalion 101, a unit of the German Order Police, who entered the Polish village of Jozefrow in the early morning of July 13, 1942. By nightfall, according to historian Christopher Browning, these rear-guard policemen too old for combat—clerks, salesmen, craftsmen, common laborers—had rounded up 1,800 Jews, separated out several hundred men as "work Jews," and shot the rest dead: some 1,500 women, children, and elderly. During the next sixteen months, these average family members, who had grown up in pre-Hitler Germany and were neither professed Nazis nor racists, obediently helped slaughter 38,000 Jews and deport 45,000 more to Treblinka's gas chamber.[1]

The conduct of the men of Police Battalion 101 is grisly proof, if needed, that the obedient action is not always the moral one. It is, nevertheless, always an action for whose outcome participants share responsibility. But, of course, "I was just following orders" would have it otherwise. This so-called Bormann defense would downplay complicity, deny culpability, and foster the delusion that noncooperation with evil is less a duty than cooperation with good. It would even make a fecund virtue of sterile loyalty, as if there were honor in robotically doing the dirty work of an evil genius.

If we were as quick to ponder why we followed orders as we are to point out that we did, we'd learn a great deal about the personal power and responsibility we're so keen to deny. We'd see "I was just following orders" for what it is: an ingenuous, if cowardly, rhetorical contrivance for gain without blame.

Why did the men of Police Battalion 101 do what they did? Why do any of us sheepishly follow orders? Why do we say yes when we should say no? Usually because we're attempting to obtain or preserve something. Whatever we're striving to get or save, then, helps explain authority's sway over us. This means that the real power lies less with the authority and more with us—with the symbolic value that *we attach* to those with power over us. So long as we perceive such figures as indispensable to our well-being, we'll follow their orders uncritically, self-persuaded that we couldn't help it. Puzzling over why we follow orders thus helps correct for the illusion of powerlessness. It stops our crying, "I couldn't help it, I was just following orders," and starts us thinking about what we could help but didn't. It reminds us that we're always accountable for which personal wants and needs—which of our various competing affections, appetites, and attachments—we let prompt our relations with authority, and to what degree.

When Christopher Browning interviewed 210 members of Police Battalion 101, he learned how much peer pressure had influenced their conduct. Now that's something all of us can relate to. Peer pressure—who hasn't felt the leaden weight of conformity influencing us this way or that? "Even in what we do for pleasure," said John Stuart Mill, "conformity is the first thing thought of":

> [People] like in crowds; they exercise choice only among things commonly done: peculiarity of taste, eccentricity of conduct, are shunned equally with crimes: until by dint of not knowing their own nature they have no nature to follow: their human capacities are withered and starved: they become incapable of any strong wishes or native pleasures, and are generally without either opinion or feelings of home growth, or properly their own.[2]

The ease with which "the mind itself is bound to the yoke," as Mill pictured our penchant to conform, helps explain but not excuse blind obedience. Mature adults understand the potentially enormous influence of peer groups on values, attitudes, and conduct. They realize that it takes strong, well considered principles and convictions of their own to stand firm against peer pressure. They accept the responsibility for distinguishing worthy from unworthy authority; legitimate from illegitimate orders; loyalty to person, party, or philosophy from loyalty to humanity. And, ultimately, grown-ups know the difference between obedient and ethical action.

Browning discovered another motive for the behavior of those "ordinary men," one as insidious and common as peer pressure: careerism. Who doesn't want to get ahead? advance in a field? rise to the top? But at what price? That's the rub. To get along some of us will go along with almost anything. In our business and professional lives, we'll bend to the yoke of the corporate will to insure the totems of success: wealth, power, social position, even hero worship. Little wonder Browning finds a sobering lesson for all of us in the ugly conduct of these "ordinary men":

> There are many societies afflicted by traditions of racism and caught in the siege mentality of war or threat of war. Everywhere society conditions people to respect and defer to authority and indeed could scarcely function otherwise. Everywhere people seek career advancement. In every modern society the complexity of modern life and the resulting bureaucratization and specialization attenuate the sense of personal responsibility of those implementing official policy. Within virtually every social collective, the peer group exerts tremendous pressure on the behavior and sets moral norms. If the men of Reserve Battalion 101 could become killers, what group of men cannot?[3]

As motivationally powerful as are peer pressure and careerism in getting us to go along, sometimes the carrot is something as simple and profound as the familiar. To some degree all of us are drawn to the familiar. But we need to be two-eyed here. It's not enough to see and enjoy only the comfort in the near and dear. We also need to recognize that what's familiar tends to become a value, and the values that sustain us derive their force from their familiarity. Psychologist Gordon Allport made exactly this point more than fifty years ago in *The Nature of Prejudice,* his monumental study of racial prejudice:

> Psychologically, the crux of the matter is that the familiar provides the indispensable basis for our existence. Since existence is good, it's accompanying groundwork seems good and desirable. A child's parents, neighborhood,

region, nation, are given to him—so too his religion, race, and social traditions. To him all these affiliations are taken for granted. Since he is part of them, and they are part of him, they are *good*.[4]

Allport's examples are of groups we're born into. But his point can be generalized to groups we join. Inclusion in religious, political, business, and professional groups help satisfy our need for the familiar. And so they too become a value, a good—sometimes so great a good that we'll ascribe goodness to whomever we perceive as representing the familiar, its conservation, and its promotion: the political leader, the religious figure, the radio host. Whoever the guru, once a bond is formed we can stop thinking for ourselves, and start following uncritically that individual's (or group's) "orders" or code, and feeling *good* about it. Thus, by emphasizing a common Aryan heritage and manufacturing threats to it—Jews and Communists, most notably—Hitler created a strong German identity. By portraying one another as imperialistic warmongers with little respect for human rights or dignity, Soviet and American cold warriors gave their respective peoples a comparably strong identity. By naming friends and enemies and prescribing particular political attitudes, religious beliefs, and social goals, the "electronic church" creates a strong "Christian identity" for its viewers.[5] By incessantly attacking liberals, "feminazis," environmentalists, and the larger portion of the working press, the fustian Rush Limbaugh has provided innumerable angry white males a palpable identity. "Once such identities form," say psychologists Anthony Pratkanis and Eliot Aronson, "the right and moral course of action becomes abundantly clear."[6] In other words, the faithful—the "ditto-heads"—are ready for their marching orders.

The point is not that we should forsake the familiar nor suppress our need to belong. Rather, it's to recognize the voracity of these needs. For the sheer warmth and comfort of a familiar place—a family, a team, a party, a religion, a corporation, a profession—we're capable of dancing to some sinister tunes. For a place in a tightly knit group fighting for common ideals, we're capable of sacrificing anything—including those ideals. In short, as Konrad Lorenz said, we're "the only being capable of dedicating [ourselves] to the very highest moral and ethical values [and at the same time capable of killing] our brother, convinced that [we're] doing so in the interests of the very same high ideals."[7]

———— •◆• ————

Acceptance, careerism, familiarity, self-identity—such is the stuff of blind obedience. Precisely because we require a measure of these things, they're good and desirable, and whoever provides them will seem worthy of our loyalty. It's up to each of us to determine the relative weight of these goods on our decision making and in our relations with authority. An overweening attachment to any of them can make those with power of authority over us seem indispensable to our well-being. Once so persuaded we're capable of uncritically following their orders or code—no matter how absurd, illegal, or immoral—and afterward stacking the deck with the unpersuasive "I was just following orders."

# 14. *"But What Else Could I Do? I Was Between a Rock and a Hard Place"*

If you saw Woody Allen's film *Crimes and Misdemeanors,* you will recall the central character: a highly successful, universally respected ophthalmologist with a loving wife and family. He also keeps a mistress, who has begun to chafe at the role of the "kept woman." Indeed, she yearns to be the physician's wife, a notion he finds as ridiculous as she does sublime. Unwilling to be bought off, the woman sets the doctor an ultimatum: Tell your wife or I will.

The prospect of discovery—of losing everything in life he has worked for and cherishes—hurtles the panicked doctor to his unsavory brother, who matter-of-factly suggests that the woman be disposed of. Murder! How dare his brother even think such a thing. Never, the physician professes, would he be party to so foul a deed. But when he intercepts a letter from his mistress to his wife, the good doctor wavers. Why, the woman is obviously out of control, dangerously deranged. She must be stopped before she destroys him. What else can he do, he decides, but have big brother ice the mistress-turned-blackmailer?

So his obliging sibling has the woman strangled by someone expert enough in these matters to make hers appear still another random urban slaying. When the doctor learns of the ugly deed, he's racked with fear and guilt. On reckless impulse he even visits the crime scene. But when, like one of his masterful surgeries, the murder passes without complication, his conscience quiets down; and the film ends where it began—with the portrait of a fabulously successful man basking in the love of his family and the esteem of his colleagues.

Happily for our potential victims, not to say an already overburdened judicial system, most of us resist our murderous impulses. But like the physician, all of us need and want some measure of approval and love, accomplishment and success, status and prestige. And having attained them, like him we fear their loss. Sometimes, in fact, the fear of losing what we profoundly crave and value, and perhaps have labored hard for, can grow strong enough to block rational thought and overwhelm considerations of common decency and respect for others. Then a titanic clash occurs between, as it were, our brighter and darker selves— between the ideal self and the real self.

The seventeenth-century French philosopher Blaise Pascal believed that this intrapsychic conflict is always with us. Pascal framed our curious predicament this way (edited for sexist pronouns):

> We want to be great, and we see ourselves as small. We want to be happy, and we see ourselves as miserable. We want to be perfect, and we see ourselves full of imperfections. We want to be the object of love and esteem among others, and we see that our faults merit only their hatred and contempt.

So what do we do?

We conceive a mortal enmity against the truth which reproves us, and which convinces us of our faults. We would annihilate it, but, unable to destroy it in its essence, we destroy it as far as possible in our own knowledge and in that of others; that is to say we devote all our attention to hiding our faults both from others and ourselves.[1]

Faced with his own imperfection and misery, the physician denies both. He lies to himself. Of course, he doesn't admit the self-deception, for that would be self-diminishing, the very thing he is attempting to avoid. Instead he finesses the self-deceit with still another, one intended to maintain his heroic stature in his own eyes: He persuades himself that he is between the proverbial rock and hard place. He can either permit his mistress to destroy him or he can destroy her. Self-persuaded of his powerlessness to do anything else but save himself by killing her, he thus concocts a recipe for the perfect crime. For not only does he get away with murder, he acquits himself before the bar of his own conscience. For where there is no freedom, there can be no responsibility, and, therefore, no blame.

History tells of another man prepared to kill, Dietrich Bonhoffer. At the outbreak of World War II, this pacifist Lutheran theologian was deeply divided. As a committed Christian he knew, like Jefferson, that resistance to tyrants is obedience to God. But to resist Nazi tyranny and oppression meant killing. So, if Bonhoffer fought, he'd violate his duty as a pacifist. But if he didn't, he'd violate his duty as a Christian. To fight or not to fight—that was the pastor's tortuous dilemma. And it was a real one, for those were his only options; he was truly between a rock and a hard place.

Bonhoffer chose to fight. He joined the underground, and was subsequently arrested, and hanged.

Life often poses such tragic options. To maintain or not maintain life support for a terminally ill loved one? To have or not to have an unwanted baby? To save or let die a massively deformed newborn? To institutionalize or not an elderly parent? To reveal or conceal from a friend the infidelity of the person's spouse? Each case poses morally good reasons for mutually exclusive alternatives—reasons like preserving life, saving pain, telling the truth, being loyal, returning favor. It's in circumstances like these—when none of the limited options yielded an entirely desirable outcome—that we always have logically and morally sound reasons to say or think: "But what else could I do? I was between a rock and a hard place." For like the priest, we too faced a genuine moral dilemma.

But often ours is not a genuine but a false dilemma. There really aren't morally good reasons for mutually exclusive alternatives. There actually are other choices, but painful ones we'd rather avoid. So we falsely reduce our options, and even manufacture "good reasons" for doing the easy but not always the more responsible thing; or for avoiding the difficult but more honorable course, and for saying retrospectively: "What else could I do? I was between a rock and a hard place."

For example, there are no good moral reasons for parents not to intervene in the lives of their drug-addicted children, although they sometimes stack the deck by persuading themselves that there are. Fear of alienating the child or losing his affection; the shame of unmasking the family as less than perfect; the guilt of complicity in the child's self-destruction—each is an excuse, but not a good reason. The same may be said generally of those who endure spousal abuse or ignore family incest. Face it: The rock and the hard place we squeeze ourselves between often has no more substance than papier-mâché, except in our own overheated and mystified minds.

Like individuals, institutions exhibit a parallel capacity for self-deceit with respect to difficult choices. How many governmental, business, educational, and religious institutions allow their options to be shaped mainly by considerations of scandal, image, or public relations? How many thus avoid the tough but right decision, and afterward attempt to dodge blame by pleading powerlessness? It has taken the Catholic Church, to cite just one example, years to openly acknowledge clerical pedophilia. Evidently fearful of giving scandal and tarnishing the Church's image, officials selected from a limited menu of misbegotten, tepid options to maintain the "family secret": stonewalling, minimizing, covering up, buying silence, transferring or counseling deviant priests. In the end, of course, the dirty little secrets came out, as they inevitably do. And with that considerations of scandal and image were revealed to be lame excuses for not doing the responsible thing: protecting vulnerable children and helping troubled priests. Even today, perhaps many church officials and laypeople console themselves with the false belief that the Church couldn't help it; it was between a rock and a hard place.

The Church, like the doctor in the movie, could have acted otherwise. It could have confronted its human failings, no matter how egregious, openly and honestly. The doctor could have borne the fury of a scorned mistress, no matter how personally damaging. The parent of the drug-addicted child can practice "tough love" and the parent of the unruly one can enforce discipline, even if it means being despised. None of this is easy to do. It requires honesty and courage, the two character traits indispensable to personal and institutional responsibility—the honesty to count the painful but right course within one's power, and the courage to take it.

———•◆•———

When the choices you face leave you disinclined to face your choices, keep in mind that the hope is not to end up with no regrets, but with the right regrets.[2]

# 15. *"The Devil Made Me Do It"*

The appeal to an overpowering, preternatural force to excuse human mischief and miscreancy is as ancient as the Bible and as contemporary as a comedy club.

The record does not show that God was amused when told by Eve after the fall: "The serpent beguiled me" (Genesis 3:13). But many of us still are when Geraldine, the character made popular in the 1970s by comedian Flip Wilson, proclaims her innocence with an indignant: "The Devil made me do it." A true daughter of our "first parents," the plucky, street-smart lady of easy virtue continues to get laughs when she plays the powerless pavement princess in the hands of the Prince of Darkness.

Had she lived in ancient Rome, Geraldine might have blamed the stars. A medieval European Geraldine or a colonial American one could have pointed a bony finger of accusation at controlling demons or witches. Such is "the excellent foppery of the world," says Shakespeare in *King Lear,* "that, when we are sick in fortune, often the surfeits of our own behavior, we make guilty of our disasters the sun, the moon, and the stars."[1]

The Bard, of course, didn't have us in mind. We moderns know better than to blame devils, stars, and witches for our failings and foul-ups. Instead we speak of the powerful influence of parents, poverty, and prejudice. Our preferred stargazers are not astrologers but psychologists who urge and help us conjure up "governing scenes," events from our childhood so powerful that they virtually determine our behavior. For the more biologically minded there are disabling genes: the "alcohol gene," the "aggression gene," the "promiscuity gene." Drink, fight, seek love in all the wrong places—bad seeds make us do it all. And let's not forget economics. How many corporate crooks and creeps are "driven" to their sleaze by competition? "Don't blame me for the filthy billboard in your backyard. Competition forced me to do it." "Don't blame me for trying to seduce you and your kids into life-destroying habits. I'm just trying to keep up with the competition."

With near unshakable conviction some students tell me they simply can't do math. Misspelling is the cruel fate of others. "I just can't spell," a thirty-something confesses with opaque fatalism. "I've never been able to." One evil gene evidently renders some lamentable souls incapable of distinguishing *to* from *too,* while another gene decrees they spell *a lot, alot.* An otherwise intelligent young woman once hinted darkly at the demon dyslexia to explain her affinity for fused sentences and comma splices. Happy to say, I successfully exorcised this devil—well, partially. The student is now a dyslexic who never writes a run-on sentence.

Modern-day demons gambol in our harried halls of justice. In one widely reported trial, the defense insisted that "racial rage" was why his client, a black man, killed several whites. In another, "urban stress syndrome" was said to have compelled a teenager to kill another teen for a leather coat. (Apparently, growing up in a violent neighborhood programs black people to fear other inner-city blacks.) "Adopted child syndrome" supposedly was why Joel Rifkin killed seventeen prostitutes. Another "syndrome" is supposed to explain why a teenage girl killed a four-year-old boy: "fetal trimethadione syndrome"—in other words, the girl's sadism was caused by medication taken by her epileptic mother during pregnancy. Today even "image" can become the defendant in the dock, as in the trial of the seventeen-year-old who killed a sixteen-year-old for the latter's $90 Nike Air Jordans. It's deplorable, the prosecution lamented, when we create such an image of luxury about athletic gear that it "forces" people to kill over it.

True, courts rarely allow defenses based on premenstrual syndrome, alcoholism, compulsive gambling, "black rage," or "urban survival syndrome." But such defenses are made, and taken together with the long list of "personality disorders" under the Americans With Disabilities Act of 1990 they tend to "medicalize character." That's a phrase coined by professor and clinical psychologist G. E. Zuriff of Wheaton College and MIT for what he views as the psychiatric profession's success in treating as disabilities emotional problems that often are within the individual's power to control and thus for which we can be held accountable.[2]

Judges aren't immune to the pandemic tendency to invoke some devil or other to excuse conduct. Under a withering barrage of criticism that extended from Main Street to Pennsylvania Avenue, in 1996 a federal judge in

New York reversed his decision suppressing a videotaped confession and a ton of evidence in a drug case. (Actually, it was only eighty pounds of cocaine and heroin found in the trunk of the defendant's car.) "Unfortunately," said the judge in explaining his self-reversal, "the hyperbole in my initial decision not only obscured the true focus of my analysis, but regretfully may have demeaned the law-abiding men and women who make Washington Heights their home and the vast majority of the dedicated men and women in blue who patrol the streets of our great city."[3] Will no one rid his Honor of this meddlesome hyperbole that obscures and demeans—not to mention that upstart, personification?

Often our demonic inner compulsions are less poetic than amorous. Take Southern California Woman—not an early female life form found stuck in the La Brea tar pits of Los Angeles, but a letter writer seeking some "clear-eyed, unbiased advice" from Ann Landers. It seems SCW is mired in an affair with her physician, "Stu." She boasts that she knows "the word on sex these days—either abstain, remain in a monogamous relationship, or use a condom under all circumstances"—and says she respects and trusts Dr. Stu, who has been with several other women. What puzzles SCW is her doctor-lover's refusal to wear a condom. She's worried that it wouldn't take much for her "good sense" to evaporate in the "heat of passionate impulse." She says she realizes she's a married woman, but she simply can't control her strong feelings. Alas, it seems that, like Geraldine, the "Devil" is about to make SCW do it.[4]

Akin to these overwhelming, devil-like inner compulsions are those equally controlling outer forces that we believe confound our lives. Topping the list, perhaps: "government," with whom we generally stand in relationship as a teenager to a parent. We want government out of our lives—"off our backs," as a former president liked to say—except, of course, when, like adolescents, we need something. If those meanies, dolts, fuddy-duddies, and borderline white-collar felons running government would just go away, or at least get out of the way, we could be free to be our most productive and profitable selves. In a word, it's the devil government that's holding us back and keeping us from getting ahead. At least that seems the sentiment of a lot of middle-class Americans today.

Not long ago a front page story entitled "For Voters, Hope Gives Way to . . . Cynicism" profiled an anesthesiologist in Savannah, Georgia, and a firefighter in Richmond, Virginia, both of whom were thinking of moving to Costa Rica to escape the "appalling" economic conditions in the United States.[5] The anesthesiologist didn't think it would be economically feasible to live in this country in ten years. Perhaps not, but he failed to mention the Medicare, Medicaid, worker's compensation payments, and fee-for-service health system that help provide him and his colleagues a most comfortable living. As for the retired fifty-three-year-old firefighter, he didn't mention disliking the taxes that help public employees like him retire earlier than most of the population.

The anesthesiologist and the firefighter are but two among a rising tide of middle-income voters who, according to public opinion polls, are angry and cynical due to uncertainty about the future and feelings of personal stagnation. Presumably, they'd rather not leave their native land; it's just that, well, the devil government is forcing them out.

Author Garrison Keillor calls these malcontents "sore-heads." "In the adult segment of your life," the humorist reminds Angry Voter, "in the part of your life that comes after your parents kiss you good-bye and kick you out, the future is always uncertain. Even in the past the future was uncertain, and it always will be. And if you don't get ahead, you aren't entitled to blame the president, the Congress, or your poor old mom and dad. This is true even in Costa Rica. I thought everybody knew that."[6]

If we're not entitled to blame government for self-stagnation, how much less may we blame it for our lack of self-control. And yet we seem to. Thus: If we cheat on our taxes, an unfair tax code forces us to. If we've become morally flaccid, a godless government has made us that way. If our public schools are failing, a curriculum crafted by sinister forces insure their failing. If economic entitlements continue to balloon, spineless, self-serving politicians keep pumping them up. What's all the political hectoring and public clamoring about government cleaning up the entertainment industry and confiscating cigarette vending machines but a pitiful admission that we can't control our kids? And what about those legislators we're beseeching to save us and our kids from ourselves? What are they up to? Why, they're trying to pass a law to stop themselves from spending more—the much-publicized budget-balancing constitutional amendment. They, too, it seems, are victims of the dreaded "system."

None of this is lost on columnist Russell Baker, who likens our hardy appetite for government to rescue us from the excesses of our own lack of self-control to the lipstick message left by the serial murderer on one victim's wall: "For heaven's sake," the killer wrote, "catch me before I kill more. I cannot control myself." For Baker "the handwriting on the wall says we are a people unable to control ourselves, a people craving government, a people who want government firmly on our back."[7]

Well, perhaps not all of us. Leaders of armed militia in thirty-nine states mince no words in denouncing and demonizing government. For them, "government is the enemy of the people," and the president—it doesn't really matter which—is a dictator. On the one hand, they say they deplore acts of terrorism; on the other, they say they understand how an "oppressive government" might drive someone to bomb the federal office building in Oklahoma City. Some of these superpatriots even hint broadly of a conspiracy at the highest levels of "government" to conceal its own involvement in the bombing. In other words, either the government was behind it or the government drove someone like Timothy McVeigh to it. (While in custody, McVeigh, incidentally, described himself as a "political prisoner.") Militia leaders warn further of an impending armed conflict between the forces of good or ordinary citizens like themselves and the forces of evil or ZOG ("Zionist Occupational Government"). They don't prophesy the outcome of this Armageddon. Perhaps their eschatology includes a brave new world when we can once and for all get the old devil government off our backs to make room for a new one—a government that will allow us to be, in the words of an erstwhile army recruitment ad, "all that we can be"—that is, perhaps, the proud possessors of live grenades and bazookas, and, for those who can afford it, a cruise missile or two.

———— • ◆ • ————

As the origin of the first misfortune of humankind, the Devil remains the mythic dark and disturbing spirit whose treacherous cunning we look for behind our failings and reversals, our crimes and inhumanities, and in our disillusionment and dystopia. But when we look, it's unlikely to be Voltaire's "black sheep of the heavenly hosts" we espy, but the haunted projection of our own enemies and fears. This is our prince of darkness, who tricks us not into doing what's forbidden, but into believing that we couldn't help it.

# 16. *"Boys Will Be Boys"*

In 1993, a flurry of publicity followed revelation that members of a southern California clique named for a professional basketball team were accused of coercing sex from girls, one as young as ten, and keeping tally. If you followed the saga of the "Spur Posse" sex-for-points scandal, you may have recognized in media accounts a stock cast of characters, including: predatory teenage boys winning status though sexual conquest; "easy," insecure girls gaining reassurance by making themselves available to popular, good-looking athletes; image-conscious school officials trying to control the fast-spreading notoriety; town pooh-bahs and boosters blaming an overly zealous media for magnifying "small indiscretions." And, of course, the boys' parents, who downplayed the whole unseemly episode with what amounted to a nonchalant "Boys will be boys," for three centuries a most serviceable proverb.[1]

In the study of logic, a statement like "Boys will be boys" is called a tautology. That means it's self-evident—as indubitable, say, as "Cats will be cats." Because tautologies cannot be logically denied, they foreclose debate. So when those parents in effect rationalized "Boys will be boys," they were not merely trivializing their sons' behavior, they were preempting any serious evaluation of it. They were really saying, "What my son did is what boys do"; and, implicatively, "He couldn't help it, and therefore is not to blame."

Now when cats chase mice we're hardly surprised. That is, after all, what the frisky feline naturally does. But what about boys like the Spur Posse bunch? Are they hard-wired to prey and pounce on girls for points? Is such behavior as much in their nature as it is in the cat's to toy with and kill a mouse? Of course not. But by its sheer logical force, the tautology "Boys will be boys" can make it seem that way. Thus, "My son simply could not have acted otherwise because he's a boy and that's what boys do." Only a fool would hold a cat accountable for pawing a mouse. By the same token, goes the logic, it's just as foolish—indeed irresponsible and unfair— to hold son (and parent) fully accountable.

What in fact is foolish—and spineless, as well—is to make such an excuse for a boy's harmful lack of self-control and for one's own equally damaging unwillingness to help instill self-discipline in him. What is irresponsible is not holding such a boy accountable for a range of behaviors from bullying to brawling to sexual assault and date rape. What is unfair, and hypocritical, is demanding that our schools be safe and orderly but not supporting them unreservedly when they lower the boom on classroom rowdies and fraternity drunks. And let's not compound the cop-out by conning ourselves that "they'll outgrow it." Better to remember that "as the twig is bent the tree inclines." Boys will be men.

Remember Paula Coughlin? She was the Navy lieutenant and helicopter pilot attacked by a bunch of the boys, a gauntlet of drunken aviators, at a Las Vegas hotel during their Twentieth Annual Convention. The original whistle blower in the Tailhook scandal, Coughlin sued the Las Vegas Hilton for not providing proper security during the bawdy event. In denying allegations of hotel negligence, Hilton attorneys suggested that Coughlin had only herself to blame. She was either naïve about what to expect at "Tailhook '91," they argued, or she willingly joined the drunken debauchery. In other words, either she should have known boys will be boys or she wanted to be one of the boys. Either way she got what she deserved.

So, presumably, did the junior enlisted woman who was groped by a chief petty officer while the two flew across country on a commercial flight. In this incident, which occurred two years after Tailhook, the woman reportedly screamed and cursed and tried to fend off the advances, while about twenty other sailors on board, including two officers—one a chaplain—did little to intercede. (An Air Force colonel finally came to the rescue.) The junior enlistee probably should have known better than to board the flight, sit next to the petty officer, or expect much help from the boys on board.

In the culture where boys will be boys, others—usually females—get what they deserve because of their own naïveté, ignorance, weakness, or choice. Even in the most extreme cases, such as wife-beating or rape, we often look for victim complicity. Why did the battered wife stay with the brutal husband? Did she really think she could change him? save the marriage? keep the family together? How naive, if not downright stupid. Why, the whole notion of staying with a batterer makes as much sense as remaining in a burning building. Or, alternatively: If she wasn't naive, she probably asked for it. Like Paula Coughlin, she got what she deserved. So either way—casting the woman as accomplice, on the one hand, or provocateur, on the other—the blame for the battering (or rape or sexual harassment) can get spread almost equally between victim and victimizer.

If we want to blame the abused female for something, let's do it for something many of us are guilty of:

- swallowing some dangerous cultural myths about so-called appropriate gender behavior
- failing to acknowledge that, irrespective of sex, some behavior is not "inappropriate"—it's wrong
- recognizing the word *inappropriate* for what it often is: a psychological euphemism for *bad, immoral,* even *evil,* as well as a linguistic sign and shaper of a culture that no longer seems to know—or cares to know—the difference between *polite* and *right,* manners and morals, etiquette and ethics.

And, most important, we share in the blame of the harassed, raped, and battered for continuing naively to derive our sense of self and success largely from such long-standing, socially sanctioned, behavior-shaping and -excusing gender scripts as "Boys will be boys."

Case in point: the astonishing popularity of the romance novel. According to *Forbes* magazine, 25 million American females are reading an average of twenty romance novels a month.[2] Why? What do so many women find so compelling?

"The hope and thrill of being 'saved' by a strong, dominant male who will take care of them and make them feel secure."[3] That at least is the opinion of psychologist Judith

Sherven and human-behavior specialist James Sniechowski. And why would such a man be attracted to so desperate a woman? "Because man as a protector-savior—Prince Charming—is compelled to save the damsel in distress. When he does, he is acknowledged as a *real* man."[4] (The wife-and-husband consulting team cite the O. J. Simpson– Nicole Brown Simpson relationship as fitting this pattern.) The "real man" of the romance novel fantasy is powerful and protective, and also sexually aggressive, dangerous, and forceful. To say that 25 million females feeding on a steady diet of romance novels feel inadequate is to deny understatement its due. Utterly powerless is more like it. And only the conquering hero can save such a female with his violent passion and brute strength, in the torrent of which she is helpless and *unaccountable*. For a woman like this, not only will boys be boys—they darn well better be!

No harmless adage, then, this centuries-old "Boys will be boys." The ease with which it trips off the tongue calls for caution. We may be stacking the deck. We may be using it to dodge rather than to discipline, to confer on our boys gender power and privilege by excusing their belches and boorishness, their acting up and aggression, their callow and calloused conduct. "Boys will be boys" may be exactly the wrong message to send them. Instead of letting them know that they can and must control themselves, we may be telling them they can't or don't have to. Rather than teaching them how to be cooperative, considerate, and caring, we may be saying: "It's okay to be selfish, insensitive, and brutish. You are, after all, a boy." In place of schooling them in the way of empathy, we may be setting them a course of sociopathy. (It's worth noting that one of the audacious Spur

Posse band was shot and killed at a rowdy Fourth of July bash in 1995. He was twenty-one.) In a word, rather than being accountable grown-ups, maybe we're being moral no-accounts.

And let's not forget our girls. For all the while we're excusing our boys for being boys, we may be blaming our girls for being girls. We may be filling their heads with those ridiculous, disempowering, and dangerous notions about themselves that permit boys to be boys even when they've become brutalizing men.

———— • ◆ • ————

"Boys will be boys"—an excuse trumped up in emergency or embarrassment. To offer it for not managing manageable misbehavior is the special corruption of parental weakness. "Choose to leave your children well instructed rather than rich," Epictetus counseled, "because the thoughts of the wise are better than the riches of the ignorant." [5]

# 17. *"I'm Too Old to Change"*

The Roman rhetorician Juvenal said it was more to be feared than death.[1] Shakespeare called it a condition "full of care . . . like winter weather . . . like winter bare."[2] For Benjamin Disraeli it was simply a "regret."[3] Given the picture of "crabbed age" etched so starkly for generations in prose and verse, it's no wonder most of us probably want to live long but not get old.

Even today old age often calls up images of being useless, out of touch, sick, lonely, poor, and stubborn—something akin, perhaps, to T. S. Eliot's "old man in a dry month/Being read to by a boy, waiting for rain."[4] TV, newspapers, magazines, and comic books do little to alter these perceptions. Together with stories, jokes, songs, and even birthday cards, they still too often dwell on the painful, empty, dangerous, and humiliating aspects of aging. Add to this a culture that generally glorifies youth, prizes the new and modern, derides tradition, fears and denies death, and equates human worth with getting and spending, and it isn't surprising if even the elderly themselves harbor many myths about old age.

An entry in the diary of Henri Amiel—that nineteenth-century Swiss thinker to whom the study of philosophy owes little but the human store a great deal—reads: "To know how to grow old is the master work of wisdom, and one of the most difficult chapters in the great art of living."[5] Knowing how to grow old *is* difficult because change is never easy, and never so difficult as in old age, a season of great and profound change. The wisdom lies in knowing what to change and what not.

Perhaps you can recall someone's saying, "Oh, well, I guess I'm just too old to change." The person may have been attempting to excuse something he said or did; or perhaps she was alibiing for a belief, an attitude, or just plain ignorance. The things we are too old to change (or so we say) range from the trifling and innocent to the harmful and hurtful—from retiring at the same time every night and having meals at the exact hour to excessive drinking and blind prejudice. Whatever the matter, "I'm too old to change" dismisses the capability of learning something new or different by virtue of mounting years, as if learning were strictly a function of age.

Although it's true that some things—language, for example—are more easily mastered at a young, impressionable age, middle and old age don't render one ineducable. What can and does, however, is something that haunts old and young alike: lack of motivation. "You're never too old to learn"—except when you have no reason to.

We learn best when we have a strong desire to, when we believe in the change the learning will bring. But once we lose our desire, we lose the dynamic stimulant for all learning and, thus, for personal change and growth. Lost, too, is the impulse to create, to care, to love, and live long and well. No doubt this is why Michelangelo, recognizing passionate desire as impetus to action, prayed that he might always desire more than he could accomplish.

Unlike the tireless Renaissance artist, individuals too old to change desire *less* than they can accomplish. They stack the deck by likening themselves to the proverbial "old dog" who can't be taught new tricks. But perhaps the new tricks elude them because they're not motivated to master them. They don't believe enough in the change to make the effort to learn. So, when such a person barks, "I'm too old to change," he probably means, "I don't want to change." He's able, but unwilling.

It was John Steinbeck who observed that it's in our nature as we grow older to protest against change, particularly change for the better. W. H. Auden went further. In his "Epilogue" to *The Age of Anxiety,* the Pulitzer Prize–winning poet wrote:

> *We would rather be ruined than change*
> *We would rather die in our dread*
> *Than claim the cross of the moment*
> *And let our illusions die.*[6]

But that we instinctively avoid change makes our capacity to change no less a power. To exercise this great power or not is ours to choose. But either way—to change or not— we're free and accountable. This means that we are as responsible for the outcomes of choosing *not* to change as for the consequences of changing, a point that "I'm too old to change" obscures by confusing choice with necessity.

Distinguishing inability from unwillingness is crucial to having power and control, two casualties of old age. Not confusing "can't" with "won't" is equally important for maintaining a keen sense of responsibility where otherwise we might feel only privilege as we age. Habitually being clear and honest about what we really don't want to do, as opposed to what we say we can't do, shifts the focus from the apparent to the real reasons behind our reluctance to learn and change. It inclines us to ask more, "*Why* don't I want to change?" and to alibi less, "I'm too old to change," or its close relation expressed by anyone at any age: "That's just the way I am."

Whenever we interrogate our unwillingness to learn and to change, we take the first step in identifying the personal gains and losses of our inertia, which ordinarily center around the familiar. And, if we're tough-minded enough, we'll also assess the impact of our refusal to change on ourselves and others—our family, for instance, or even the larger community. Is it helping or hurting these relationships? Is it, perhaps, alienating others and isolating us? The ancient Stoics—Seneca comes to mind—taught that it is "the worst of ills to leave the number of the living before you die."[7] Insofar as a stubborn resistance to needed change can distance and divide, leaving one morosely marooned on self-made shoals, it is indeed an extreme evil.

Avoiding this fate—the extreme evil of premature departure—isn't easy as one ages. Faced with retirement, the death of friends and loved ones, diminished health and faculties, one can easily feel unregarded and thrown in corners.[8] Challenged to keep apace of a rapidly changing world, the idle and ignored elderly can feel inadequate and obsolete. Depression can set in, even self-destructive patterns of behavior, such as alcoholism. Obviously, whatever our stage of life, there are always things we have no or little control over. But as we age we can unwittingly participate in the extreme evil of premature departure by viewing loneliness, melancholy, irritability, and despair as preordained states of the aging process.

On the other hand, we can react as mature, responsible adults—like a widow acquaintance who, after her children moved away and her husband died, withdrew some of her emotional capital and reinvested it in new relationships and activities. Now seventy-two-year-old "Margaret" is doing things she's never done before, such as square dancing and creative writing. She's also reaching out to others because she believes that as long as she can contribute she should: She's volunteering in student learning. A wife and mother as long as she can remember, Margaret is today constantly surprising herself, and provides a splendid example of Simone de Beauvoir's "one solution if old age is not to be an absurd parody of our former life." In *The Coming of Age* the French writer urged us to

> go on pursuing ends that give our existence meaning—devotion to individuals, to groups or to causes, social, political, intellectual or creative work. . . . One's life has value so long as one attributes value to the life of others, by means of love, friendship, indignation, compassion.[9]

Doubtless thousands of other "Margarets" are similarly "coming of age," but probably not enough. If too many senior citizens who can do more don't do more—for themselves and others—maybe it's because they aren't always expected or permitted to. Perhaps we're too quick to retire our seniors, isolate them from other age groups, discourage their involvement in change-demanding activities, and insist that they "act their age." If so, we shouldn't be surprised to find many of them living more in a congenial past than in an unwelcoming present.

Juxtaposed to this forced isolation, but equally as harmful, is a sentimental indulgence of the "senior citizen," composed equally of irrational guilt and cheap pity. We frequently coddle and patronize elderly people, and think we're being charitable. We write off their displays of impatience, irritability, and incivility to "growing old," and believe we're being tolerant. We permit too many seniors to drive drugged, but punish anyone else if they do. We assume that most seniors are borderline indigents deserving of special treatment when, as a group, they have the most disposable income. And we treat the unvarnished bigotries and crass insensibilities of some of our seniors as if they were old-age perks. (How many of us, for example, sit still at family gatherings while a senior relative or two spouts off about this group or that, totally insensitive to the possibility that not everyone present might share his or her nasty prejudices or might even be offended by them?) In short, if too many seniors exploit their age to avoid needed learning and change, perhaps we're abetting them. If too many of them see only the entitlements of senior citizenship and none of its special responsibilities, maybe it's because we share their perverse belief that at some ordained age—sixty? sixty-five? seventy?—one's dues as a good citizen are paid in full.

———— • ◆ • ————

"I'm too old to change" isn't only about a stubborn resistance to learning something new or different as we grow old. Nor is it only about some senior's socially sanctioned refusal to acknowledge and take responsibility for attitudes, actions, and circumstances well within his or her power to influence. It's also about dying before one's time by living halfheartedly the time one has left. In this respect, "I'm too old to change" is about all of us who refuse to live by refusing to change; for "to change is to mature, [and] to mature is to go on creating oneself endlessly."[10]

# Part II

Embracing Personal
Responsibility

# Introduction: Mainsprings of Responsibility

If any historical figure could rightly say, "I didn't do it," it would be Socrates, who was sentenced to die after being unjustly accused of blasphemy and corrupting the young. So outraged by the shameful injustice was one of his friends that he tried to persuade "this wisest man of the ages" to escape. But Socrates refused. According to Plato in the *Crito,* a short and perennial dialogue in the literature of social protest, Socrates told his well-meaning friend: "The really important thing is not to live, but to live well. . . . And . . . to live well means the same as to live honorably or rightly."[1] Shortly afterward Socrates drank the poison hemlock and died.

For Socrates, living honorably meant abiding by the laws and judgments of the state. It also meant never returning a wrong and always practicing what one preaches—having integrity. Because his punishment had been legally decided, Socrates believed that to flee from it would be wrong and inconsistent with everything he stood for and taught.

Was Socrates right in his judgment? Was his decision justified? Or, given the trumped-up charges, did he have excellent reason to escape? Whatever one's personal judgment about Socrates—and philosophers themselves disagree—

his decision remains, in Bill Bennett's words, "one of history's great examples of an individual who believes his first responsibility to his community, his family, and himself is to follow the dictates of reason-directed conscience."[2]

Few of us are ever summoned to die for our beliefs, and were we, perhaps only a tiny fraction would. But all of us can become more Socratic by continually moving in the direction of increased self-responsibility. We can learn to "live well"—rightly and honorably—by avoiding responsibility less and embracing it more. But how?

Certainly becoming more sensitive to and less tolerant of one's own language of excuse and evasion is a good beginning. For if, as George Orwell believed, language is "an instrument which we shape for our own purposes,"[3] then language of avoidance can be viewed as an effect of our own self-serving designs. Not wanting to take full responsibility for our lives, we create expressions of self-excuse. But practiced enough, as Orwell also observed, an effect can become a cause. "Cop-out" language can "make" us cop out. To reverse the process isn't easy—changing habits never is. But if we're willing to take the trouble, we can learn to stop using expressions of evasion and excuse, and thereby think more clearly about personal responsibility. Alternatively, when we do use such expressions, we can stop and think of how we may be saying: "I didn't do it," when we did; "I didn't know it," when we should have; or "I couldn't help it," when we could have.

But language alone isn't the answer any more than it alone is the problem. Neither are good intentions, random acts of kindness, or daily affirmations. In the end, expressions of evasion and avoidance like the preceding ones reflect an immaturity rooted in a mixed blend of the psychological, the social, and the spiritual. So, ultimately, they need addressing on those levels.

For example, like most other things in life, we'll be responsible only insofar as we're motivated to be. To the degree that we're persuaded that disowning best serves us, we'll continue to duck responsibility. So to call avoiding personal responsibility partly a psychological problem is to acknowledge motivation as a key component of owning and owning up to our actions.

Now one of the most powerful stimulants to self-responsibility is caring about others. Where there's no social interest—no genuine concern for the well-being of others, but only self-absorption—there's no basis for community and no stimulant to personal responsibility. Indeed, a lacking in social interest stands the whole notion of responsibility on its head. So to say that avoiding personal responsibility is partly a social problem is to acknowledge social interest as a second key component of owning and owning up to our actions.

But avoiding self-responsibility isn't merely a matter of weak motivation and social interest—it's not only a psychological and social problem. It's also—indeed, perhaps, largely—a problem of the spirit. In other words, it's at least as much a problem of how we respond to the world as it is of caring enough about its inhabitants to honor and respect them, as the following incident illustrates.

In an interview with telejournalist Bill Moyers, philosopher of religion Jacob Needleman described what happened during the launch of *Apollo 17*, at which he was a participant observer: Minutes before the launch, hundreds of cynical reporters are milling about drinking beer and wisecracking. Then the countdown comes, and the dazzling liftoff of the thirty-five-story-high, white rocket. Suddenly you can almost hear the jaws of the reporters dropping. As the spacecraft rises, slowly and majestically, a sense of wonder consumes everyone present. Higher and higher *Apollo* ascends until it becomes a bright dot, like a star in the heavens—but with a startling difference. There are humans on it. And then there is silence. In the following words Needleman described what happens next: "The people just get up quietly, helping each other up. They're kind, they open doors, they look at each other, speaking quietly and interestedly. They were suddenly moral people because wonder, the sense of wonder, the experience of wonder, had made them moral."[4]

Even those of us never privileged to witness the launch of a spacecraft firsthand may have experienced a similar feeling of wonder, perhaps at the end of a play or film, in a religious service, at the birth of a child, on a nature trail, or even in the midst of a tragedy. Like the observers of *Apollo,* we too may have felt that awe, that "contemplation of mystery," as Lewis Mumford termed it, that brings people together and makes them naturally sharing and caring.

Perhaps the sense of wonder has this humanizing effect on us because it fills us with humility and reverence. We sense our limits and vulnerabilities; we feel a profound respect, even love. Where there is this experience of wonder or surprise, there's also understanding, both cognitive and affective: Meaning or significance is perceived, empathy is felt, then tolerance follows. *Humility, reverence, understanding, empathy, tolerance*—no wonder that wonder makes us moral. It's a spiritual power that turns the mind and heart; and like Wordsworth's "one impulse from a vernal wood," wonder can teach us more "of man/Of moral evil and of good,/Than all the sages can."[5]

To say that avoiding personal responsibility is partly a problem of the spirit, then, is to say that too many of us have lost this humanizing sense of wonder that is essential for responding maturely to our world and its inhabitants. To much of what life offers, our response is a cynical "Been there, done that"; or an impatient "Cut to the chase" or "So what's the bottom line?" Above all else we want to know what's in it for us, because, above all else, we value our physical well-being and worldly possessions.

So long as we respond to life with fashionable cynicism and see it as no more than froth and bubble, life will offer us little else. So long as we remain closed to any but the most superficial and shallow disclosures of the world, life will lack depth and our lives substance. So long as we can't be moved by life, life won't matter and we won't count. And so long as we lack a sense of wonder, we'll be lacking what makes us "open doors," "look at each other," and "speak quietly and interestedly."

———•◆•———

The remainder of this modest work discusses seven prescriptions for avoiding responsibility less and embracing it more. Some address the psychological aspects of growing a sense of self-responsibility, others the social or spiritual. No one of them is easy to practice or ever completely finished, no more than living responsibly is. Each is an ongoing part of the life's work of one who, like

Socrates, is more interested in "living well" than in merely living. View these prescriptions, then, as both basic responsibilities we have as mature adults and as ways to become more mature and responsible. Taken together they constitute some "mainsprings of responsibility."

# 18. *Recasting Your Fear*

What we fear we avoid, and the more we fear it the more we avoid it. That, in a nutshell, explains our many inventions for avoiding personal responsibility. It's also why we need to recast our fear of responsibility to be more responsible. Until we reappraise, challenge, and understand our fear, we can't own and own up to our actions.

Learning not to fear responsibility isn't easy because of the negative associations it has in our minds. One of the earliest lessons we learn, and later repeat, is that standing behind our behavior can be risky business. It can get us in trouble, when disowning might keep us out of it. It can cost us power, position, and privilege, when disowning might insure and enlarge them. It can make us unliked and unwanted, when disowning could keep us popular. And owning up can cause us to be anxious and uncertain, when disowning would sedate us. It's this expectation of blame, pain, and punishment, then, that we fear about responsibility and need to recast. We need to reappraise the fear-provoking aspects of responsibility, challenge its associations with misery, and ultimately use the power of our understanding to deflate our fear of taking responsibility and inflate our fear of avoiding it.

Ralph Waldo Emerson said that "fear always springs from ignorance."[1] If we fear more than favor self-responsibility, perhaps it's because we don't fully understand it. We know its price but not its value. We see the bad it can bring but not the good it makes possible. We're persuaded that owning up can limit our happiness but never realize that disowning places happiness off-limits, not only for ourselves, but for the children we may be cuing to shift the blame, play dumb, or stack the deck.

Perhaps if we chased it less and pondered it more, we'd realize that happiness depends entirely on responsibility— that happiness, not misery, is the true mate of responsibility. We would understand, for example, that in order to be happy we need to know that our lives have meaning. But meaning requires freedom. Only if we're free to think and choose and act for ourselves can our lives be meaningful in any meaningful sense. But freedom means responsibility. Each of us is free only to the degree that we stand behind what we do. This means that every outcome falsely disowned is freedom rejected. Every action falsely ascribed to controlling forces is meaning vacated. And every shifting of blame, playing dumb, or pleading powerless is happiness lost.

We'd understand, too, that if we need freedom and meaning to be happy, we also need love. In *The Phenomenon of Man,* his best-known work, French theologian Pierre Teilhard de Chardin wrote: "Love alone is capable of uniting living beings in such a way as to complete and fulfill them, for it alone takes them and joins them by what is deepest in themselves."[2] Thornton Wilder expressed a like sentiment in the last lines of his novel, *The Bridge of San Luis Rey:* "There is a land of the living and a land of the dead and the only bridge is love, the only survival, the only meaning."[3] Philosopher and poet alike, then, remind us of what modern psychology confirms: We need to love and be loved for both health and happiness.

To the question "What is love?" sages have offered a galaxy of answers. Indeed, as the saying goes, love is probably the only thing about which it's impossible to say anything absurd. And yet in all the many definitions of *love* there is one constant: a deep and active concern for the loved one—in other words, a sense of responsibility. So whatever else it may be, to love is to be accountable for another's well-being. When we love (and are loved) in this self-surrendering, humanizing way, we don't insure happiness. But when we don't, we insure its absence.

The fear-breeding ignorance of the child who shirks responsibility is understandable. Young and unformed, the child naturally sees happiness strictly as the presence of pleasure and the absence of pain. Self-absorbed in the extreme, the young girl or boy is a long way from realizing with George Bernard Shaw that "we have no more right to consume happiness without producing it than to consume wealth without producing it."[4] But come adulthood, childish notions need to be swept aside. "I didn't do it," "I didn't know it," and "I couldn't help it" need to be unmasked as dangerous imposters that appear to be moving us closer to the happiness we seek and deserve but, in fact, are taking us away from it. And happiness needs to be understood not in terms of some infantile and basely simplistic pleasure/pain principle but for what it actually is: a complex good whose key constituents—meaning, freedom, and love—are only attainable by living responsibly.

———•◆•———

In what does recasting our fear of responsibility simply consist? In no more and no less than replacing the childish fiction that responsibility means misery with the adult truth that the limits of personal responsibility are the limits of personal happiness.

# 19. *Knowing Yourself*

Echoing the teaching of the ancients, Pascal writes in *Pensées:* "One must know oneself. If this does not serve to discover truth, it at least serves as a rule of life, and there is nothing better."[1]

Certainly there is no more necessary rule for responsible living than to know what we feel, think, and believe; to be aware of the factors that contribute to our emotions, thoughts, and beliefs; to know who and what have influenced our attitudes, values, and habits—why we choose one thing instead of another, or follow, perhaps, the more rather than the less traveled path. If we care at all about personal freedom, we owe ourselves such knowledge, for only by understanding the what and why of who we are can we take charge of those outer forces and inner compulsions that otherwise will rule our lives. With self-knowledge we lay the groundwork for the inner life without which we're slave to chance and circumstance. If knowledge is power, then self-knowledge—together with self-discipline and self-reverence—truly is the "sovereign power" Tennyson said it was.[2]

But we don't owe it only to ourselves to know ourselves. We also owe self-insight and -understanding to others, as we owe them our moral maturity. "The questions which one asks oneself," said James Baldwin, "begin, at last, to illuminate the world, and become one's key to the experience of others."[3] In other words, self-knowledge is the window into one's moral development, into the origins and sources of one's sense of right and wrong, fair and foul. Only with moral self-insight do we meet and test our deepest moral beliefs, identify moral blind spots, and consciously choose the course to follow in order to live socially more mature lives.

So at the very time "Know yourself" is taking us inward, it's turning us outward. It is these two dimensions—the one personal, the other social—that make "Know yourself" a solid rule of life and the centerpiece of personal responsibility. And it's the fact that knowing oneself is always a work in progress, a continuous process, a life's career that is never completed once and for all that makes self-knowledge—in Cicero's words—"the most difficult thing in the world."[4]

Although self-knowledge may pose an enormous challenge, it's not an impossible one. In fact, there are many things all of us can do to become more self-knowing about our attitudes and commitment to personal responsibility. We can, for example, become better observers of what we say and do. We can look for language of avoidance in our emotional responses to criticism—signs of shifting the blame, playing dumb, and pleading powerless. We can monitor our performance in simple everyday activities, as well as in complex roles. How do we react when someone cuts us off on the highway? Do we view it as a personal affront and respond in kind, perhaps by tailgating for a few miles? Or do we frame the maneuver as the careless and unintentional action of a harried and hurried motorist—an uneventful reminder, perhaps, to drive extra defensively and considerately? What about our performance as spouses, parents, neighbors, and workers? How dutiful are we? The extent of our fidelity to the canons of a particular role or activity can teach us a great deal about our attitude toward self-responsibility. So can looking for harmony between our words and actions—integrity. Do we act as we exhort? practice what we preach? walk the talk? One author on the subject says that any self-knowledge inventory would be incomplete without answering at least the following questions about ourselves:

> How trustworthy am I? Can I keep a secret or must I reveal it to at least one or two others? Am I loyal to my friends? Do I ever "use" people? How sensitive am I to the feelings of others? Do I ever purposely hurt others? Am I jealous of anyone? Do I enjoy causing trouble, sowing seeds of suspicion and dissension among people? Do I rush to spread the latest gossip? Do I talk behind my friends' backs? Are my comments about others usually favorable or unfavorable? Do I criticize others' real or imagined faults as a means of boosting my own ego? Do I keep my promises? How tolerant am I of people's faults and mistakes?[5]

As we're taking stock of ourselves with regard to personal responsibility, let's not overlook the social environment. For example, things about other people that really get under our skin can be opportunities for becoming more knowing about our own sense of self-responsibility. Here's how it can work: Think of something that really boils your blood. Pinpoint why, then ask yourself: "In what ways am I no different?" For example, lots of us resent welfare cheats. Why? Probably because they're taking something for nothing. Fair enough, but are *we?* Maybe we're cheating at work or play, on our taxes, tests, applications, and insurance claims. We may not be cheating on our spouses, but perhaps we're taking more than giving to the relationship. If we're taking too much for granted in our lives, then we too are taking something for nothing. In that sense, we're like the welfare cheat we despise.

Again, politicians certainly drive many of us up the wall. Why? ("Let me count the ways," you may be thinking.) Topping the list might be what we view as their crass and callous disregard of anyone's interests but their own. Okay, but how are we, perhaps, as selfish as some politicians are? In what aspects of *our* lives are we self-absorbed? In what ways are *we* looking out strictly for Number 1? How many times have *we* asked, "What's in it for me?" or wondered, "What can I get away with?" If we've ever made someone look bad to make ourselves look good, we should recognize only too well opportunism in the politicians we rail against. They are, after all, like us.

And what about all those lawyers and judges we love to hate? those proceduralists versed more in the letter than the spirit of the law? Doesn't it just infuriate you to see some of them so concerned about the rights of criminals? It does me. Then again, I'm not always above searching for the small print and loopholes of life to dodge the bullet of blame. Anyone whose only defense ever was a bald "It's legal, isn't it?" or "I got a right, don't I?" is a shirttail relative, if not a first cousin, of those lawyers and jurists we delight in damning.

Of course, behind everything we say or do is a reason, albeit at times furtive and complex. Although we can come to know a great deal about what we are without knowing why, understanding the contributing factors can throw additional light on our attitude toward responsibility. It can retrieve subtle and long-forgotten lessons we learned about responsibility and expose the distant roots of present behavioral patterns of evasion and avoidance. Such insight is the basis for self-improvement, self-forgiveness, and self-respect—all of which we owe ourselves and those whose lives our lives touch.

Of the many factors that bear on how we feel, think, and act, none is more important than our self-concept, that private mental picture of the self that includes feelings and beliefs about the kind of person we are and the one we believe we could or should be. Developmental psychology teaches that as young children—well before we're fully aware of what's happening—we begin to develop an opinion of ourselves as being basically good, competent, intelligent, and worthy; or basically bad, inadequate, unintelligent, and unworthy. We draw these opinions from the cues of parents, teachers, close friends, and whoever else is important to us. The mental image of ourselves we ultimately internalize not only influences how we see ourselves in relation to others—for example, competent or incompetent—but it also affects how we treat them. In other words, how much care and concern we show for others, as well as for our own character and conduct, is partly a function of our self-concept. There is, then, a relationship between one's self-concept and one's sense of self-responsibility that's worth exploring. It may help explain why we're perhaps avoiding responsibility more than embracing it.

Take as an admittedly simplified example the case of a woman who, as a child, could never quite please her parents.

Putting aside for purposes of illustration considerations of race, religion, economics, and other powerful influences on her self-concept, let's just focus on this one key fact of her upbringing: No matter how hard she tried, she could never entirely please Mom and Dad. Perhaps she even suffered by relentless comparison to a sibling or felt inadequate to save her parents' troubled marriage. In any event, as she grew up in a culture of strict gender roles and expectations, like many other females she was further socialized to attribute failure to personal defects and success to luck.

Now it's not so surprising that this always-made-to-feel-inadequate little girl eventually grows into an extremely controlling and self-blaming woman. Constantly trying to boost her own ego, she's hard-pressed to acknowledge the needs of other egos. Thus, rather than sincerely congratulating family and friends on jobs well done, she's more likely to strike an "I told you so" pose, as in: "Didn't I tell you you could do it?" thereby alienating others by making their accomplishment her success. But if this woman seeks unearned credit, she also takes undeserved blame. As self-demanding as she is controlling, she insures her sense of basic inadequacy by holding herself to unrealistic standards and expectations. As a result, she always seems to be blaming herself, even for things outside her control. She's convinced that whatever happens at home or work, in her private or public life, is always her fault. She's learned that by taking the blame she saves conflict and gets sympathy, but is less aware of the guilt and shame it brings. That she is buying into the immaturity of others also escapes her, as much as the fact that she offends them by purloining their triumphs. She never notices, for example, that the more she apologizes the less *they* do. Ironically, then, in taking the blame for what she can't control, this woman consistently discounts aspects of a problem or relationship she *can* control, such as how much responsibility her family and coworkers will take for making things work. No longer able to distinguish rational from irrational self-blame, she eventually loses the rudder of responsibility. She comes to feel powerless to affect anything, while at the same time feeling responsible for everything.

This self-blaming woman's husband is just the opposite. As much as she blames herself for everything, he rarely holds himself at fault. If she was raised to feel she *had* to be Little Miss Perfect, he was raised to feel he *was* Little Mister Perfect. Like many men, he learned to attribute his success to personal qualities, while writing his failures off to "bad luck," uncontrollable circumstances, or even other people. Actually, his parents set him on this course of internalizing success and externalizing failure by underdisciplining and overindulging him as a child. Rarely enforcing fair and firm limits, they raised him as the "perfect child," the one who could do no wrong. Predictably enough, the spoiled little boy became the whining blameless man—a "King Baby"[6]—who is only too happy to have his self-blaming wife continually take him off the hook of responsibility. And, thus, the more she says "I'm sorry," "How did I fail?" "What did I do wrong?" the more he says: "I didn't do it," "I didn't know it," "I couldn't help it." In short, the more she gives, the more he takes.

If mature adults own and own up to their actions, neither of these individuals is very mature. She has learned to blame herself too much; in other words, she owns up to things she didn't do or at least isn't solely to blame for. He, on the other hand, blames himself too little—he doesn't own up to things he did or at least contributed to. She's assuming she has power and control where she doesn't; he's denying power and control where he has both. She feels too guilty; he doesn't feel guilty enough. Each is being immature. Both need to understand how their respective self-concepts are negatively influencing their sense of responsibility. They owe it to themselves, their social relationships, and especially their children, whom they're probably teaching to make excuses, cover up, and blame the other guy.

But this couple needs to be careful, as we all do. For if a little knowledge is a dangerous thing, what we discover and uncover about ourselves can be downright lethal: If we're not cautious, we can permit what we find out to kill our sense of self-responsibility. That's exactly what happens when, discovering the unpleasant, tragic, and perhaps even cruel truths about ourselves, we then abuse these facts as excuses. Self-knowledge, remember, is supposed to help us slip the bonds of inner compulsions and outer forces, not tie us to them in other ways. It's supposed to make us not less but more accountable—not for the past that we couldn't control but for the present and future we can influence. Knowing oneself makes improving oneself possible, but it doesn't guarantee it. Merely because the woman and man in our example gain self-awareness doesn't necessarily mean they'll change and grow. They may simply pout, "Well, that's just how I am" or "I've always been this way" or "That's how I was raised" or "It's too late to change now." If they do, then they will merely be multiplying their immaturity, for part of being a responsible adult is acting on self-discoveries—it is insight-based *living*, not excusing.

No adult today can seriously say, "I don't know what to do to know myself better." The mountain of readily available help for understanding ourselves better—physically, emotionally, intellectually, spiritually—is staggering. Much of it as near as the local library or bookstore, and occasionally the TV and PC. Then, too, there's the army of helping professionals: teachers, therapists, pastoral counselors, self-help groups. Beyond this is the treasure trove of cross-cultural and -generational literature, poetry, and philosophy whose wisdom is, as Ben Jonson said of Shakespeare, "not of an age but of all time."[7] In short, the help we need to know ourselves better is all there for the reading, viewing, listening, absorbing, and, most important, for the practicing. But do we have the "three Ds"—desire, discipline, and determination—to tap and deploy these resources? Do we know enough to know how to learn? That's another matter entirely.

"Nothing in the world is so distasteful to man as to go the way which leads him to himself," Hermann Hesse wrote in *Demian*.[8] We dread self-knowledge for the same reason George Bernard Shaw said we dread freedom—both mean responsibility.[9] But the alternative—ignorance of self—is to be dreaded more because it deprives us of the only real power any of us has: the power to take full responsibility for our lives. But as power-limiting as self-ignorance can be, it no more confers peaceful innocence in life than it does safe passage through it. What we don't know *can* hurt us, and what we should know can convict us. Self-ignorance is no excuse.

"The unexamined life is not worth living,"[10] said Socrates, a declaration that Thomas Szasz amended. According to the famous psychiatrist, "We should pledge ourselves to the proposition that the irresponsible life is not worth living either."[11] Together—the vigilance of Socrates and the accountability of Szasz—make up the whole meaning of "Know yourself." Admittedly a hard doctrine to practice, this often quoted and underhearkened adage doesn't allow us to blame "devils" and make scapegoats for our own miscues and misdeeds. Nor does it permit us to wallow in self-pity for what may have happened to us when we were young and vulnerable, innocent and overly trusting. Self-pity is not self-responsibility, and self-knowledge that ends in self-pity is sentimental self-justification. Better we never gain any self-insight than use it to pity ourselves and manipulate others. At least then we can remain innocent of knowing better than we do, albeit guilty of not knowing at all.

# 20. *Letting Your Conscience Be Your Guide, Not Your God*

It's commonplace to think of the conscience as a "little voice inside us." This "compass of the unknown" supposedly tells us what's right and wrong, accuses and blames, and never acquits the guilty. When we heed it, says Shakespeare, a still and quiet conscience promises "a place above all earthly desire."[1] When we don't, another poet warns, "Nor ear nor tongue can tell/The tortures of that inward hell." In less Byronic terms: Even if it doesn't stop us from doing something, conscience generally keeps us from enjoying it.

Of course, the individual conscience isn't literally an "inner voice." Like the self-concept, it evolved gradually in us as we slowly incorporated the culturally drenched moral lessons and rules of our parents and others. What we call our conscience, then, basically comprises the many moral associations we've made in growing up.

These conscience-forming moral lessons and connections also give us our earliest and foundational sense of personal responsibility. For example, as children most of us probably were taught to tell the truth and never to steal. Our obedience was rewarded, our disobedience punished. It is roughly thus that we initially come to associate responsibility with pleasing others: As children we learn that what we ought to do is meet the expectations of those with power of authority over us.

As we mature, our motivations can (and should) grow more complex, our self-understanding more insightful. If we so choose, we can reflect on our earliest moral lessons. We can *question* authority; *expand* our sense of personal responsibility beyond the narrow limits of reward and punishment, social convention, and conformity; *consciously make* new connections; or *strengthen* the old ones. We can do all of this, or we can remain morally arrested. In other words, we can remain unconscious of what we've absorbed long before we knew what we were absorbing—we can allow reward and punishment, pleasure and pain, to define the extent of our responsibility. In the end the choice comes down to staying a child or growing up.

Given the way conscience and a sense of self-responsibility develop, advice like "Always follow your conscience" isn't always helpful or even benign. That "still small voice" may be giving us permission to do what isn't right but, perhaps, merely gratifies our ego, pleases others, complies with orders, advances our careers, proves our loyalty, makes us popular, advances a cause, preserves our self-esteem, happens to be legal, or seems "such a small thing." Then what we're hearing is more the "invention of the devil"[2] than "the soft whispers of God."[3]

By the same token, counsel like "Never go against your conscience" can mislead by making of oneself the sole judge of good and evil. Because conscience, like judgment, can err,[4] that "inner voice" may be prompting us to avoid doing the right thing, or torturing us for doing it. This is exactly what Huck Finn discovered on a raft on the Mississippi with his friend the runaway slave Jim.[5] Recall the poignant and powerful scene when, reaching the place where Jim will be set free, Huck starts feeling guilty about helping his friend escape:

> It hadn't ever come home to me before, what this thing was that I was doing. But now it did; and it stayed with me, and scorched me more and more. I tried to make out to myself that *I* warn't to blame, because *I* didn't run Jim off from his rightful owner; but it warn't no use, conscience up and says, every time, "But you knowed he was running for his freedom, and you could a paddled ashore and told somebody." That was so—I couldn't get around that, noway. That was where it pinched. Conscience says to me, "What had poor Miss Watson done to you, that you could see her nigger go off right under your eyes and never say one single word? What did that poor old woman do to you that you could treat her so mean? . . ." I got to feeling so mean and so miserable I most wished I was dead.[6]

Huck's defining experience isn't about ignoring conscience. It's about not treating conscience as an infallible voice of moral authority.

Huck picked up his principles and prejudices where all of us do: in his own backyard, his childhood world. It's easy to forget this and treat the dictates of conscience as immutable laws of nature, whereas they derive from custom. And custom, as Huck learned, can be a source of error and an enemy of independent thought. "The principal effect of the power of custom," said Montaigne, "is to seize and ensnare us in such a way that it is hardly within our power to get ourselves back out of its grip and return into ourselves to reflect and reason about its ordinances."[7] In other words, the common notions we acquire as children or find in vogue around us can seem "universal and natural ones"—even slavery. And so, what challenges custom—what is off its "hinges," as Montaigne put it—"people believe to be off the hinges of reason."[8]

———— • ◆ • ————

The opinions and customs we have absorbed in growing up, the ones we hold and practice, may be rational or irrational, fair or biased, liberating or diminishing. So can our conscience. Being responsible, therefore, is heeding but not hypnotically following the "inner voice" of conscience. It is challenging that voice, critically conversing with it, and always pressing it into discourse with other consciences. Anything less sullies this most ennobling of our attributes by treating a sterling guide as a tin god.

# 21. *Thinking As a Member of the Moral Community*

There is a "plumb-line" which, though "as native to humanity as breathing or the upright gait," we must learn or perish.[1] The "plumb-line" or law that Alfred Adler had in mind when he expressed this sentiment is the one expressed in Leviticus 19:18: "Thou shalt love thy neighbor as thyself." In essence "the Golden Rule," this moral maxim expresses an ideal found in all the great religions of the world. In enjoining us to show the same concern for others as we naturally do for ourselves, the Golden Rule is a perfect way to inform and discipline conscience. But it's more than that: The Golden Rule is good medicine for the moral sickness of self-absorption.

"The least pain in our little finger gives us more concern and uneasiness than the destruction of millions of our fellow beings."[2] Perhaps the nineteenth-century essayist William Hazlitt was having a bad day when he made this judgment of humanity. Still, there's no mistaking the natural human tendency to put self first. There's no exaggerating our capacity for rationalizing our worst conduct. And there's no denying that in order to promote and protect our egos, we're quite adept at persuading ourselves that narrow self-interest is the common good, blind prejudice is righteous principle, and cold indifference is warm concern. This is why we need the Golden Rule—to ward off the self-obsession that underlies so much excuse, avoidance, self-deceit, and human misery. The rule truly is a golden one for personal responsibility because it captures the essence of responsible living: a like concern for self *and* other.

But who is our "neighbor," this individual we're urged to love as ourselves? Commenting on the history of the word *neighbor,* one dictionary says, "Loving one's neighbor as oneself would be much easier, or perhaps much more difficult, if the word *neighbor* had kept to its etymological meaning of 'near dweller.' " Modern English retains this original meaning of "near dweller," even though "one can now have many neighbors whom one does not know, a situation that would have been highly unlikely in earlier times."[3]

It *is* difficult, as the dictionary says, to love people we don't even know. It's even more difficult when those people are distant from us in time, place, or circumstance. Then the keenest of moral imaginations is called for—an uncommon empathy. And yet, in another sense, it may be easier to love the abstract distant dweller than the person next door—easier, as longshoreman-philosopher Eric Hoffer once put it, to love humanity than your neighbor. In any event, perhaps it's the vagueness of *neighbor* that makes the Golden Rule a maxim that probably is more preached than practiced. This may also help explain why many of us treat the timeless imperative as we do most commandments: We adapt it to our own individual needs and designs. We pick and choose the neighbors to love so that, in the end, they are more our own reflection than the "fellow human beings"

St. Matthew intended when he urged love of one's "neighbor" (Matthew 19:19).

The more factionalized our society becomes, the more it
seems one's individual circle of otherly concern tends to
contract. The more we huddle in interest groups, fearful
and suspicious of "outsiders," the more our notion of
"neighbor" shrinks and tightens. Eventually these organized
bodies of self-interested parties can come to mark the outer
borders of our "neighborhoods." The "neighbors" we love
become less and less the apostle's "fellow human beings" and
more and more the sociologist's "fellow community members," as in the "black" or "white community," the "Latino" or
"Anglo community," the "Christian" or "Jewish community,"
the "inner-city community," the "gay community," the "handicapped community," the "medical community," the "business community," even the "Hollywood community." If
friendliness, compassion, and support are "neighborly" feelings, then it is primarily within these social, political, economic, professional, and religious groups that a good many
of us today experience and express feelings of neighborhood. It's largely our friends, allies, and kindred spirits
whom we consider our "fellow beings" and "love" as ourselves—which is to say we narcissistically love in them our
reflected egos. Amidst all this social factionalization, "Love
thy neighbor as thyself" can transmogrify from a law of self-
lessness to one of selfishness, from altruism to egoism, from
loving concern to callous disregard. And with it, "personal
responsibility" can become a code term for "Look out
strictly for Number 1."

Alexander Solzhenitsyn once said that it was time to
remember that the first thing we belong to is humanity. The

Russian Nobel Prize winner was reminding us of a community that we rarely hear, speak, read, or write about, but is nonetheless critical to restoring the Golden Rule and to growing a mature sense of self-responsibility: the *moral* community.

In the moral community we are "neighbors" not by common fears, aspirations, background, skin color, politics, religion, or any other accidental feature, but by our common humanity. The "neighborhood" we belong to is not defined geographically, but morally, for the neighborhood of the moral community includes everyone who stands to gain or lose by our actions. Granted, it's not easy or convenient to bear in mind the potentially enormous social impacts of what we do or don't do. It's simpler and more comfortable to view our behavior as personal and private, or perhaps affecting only a few others. But that's not always true. Like a stone dropped into a pond, our actions make ripples, sometimes far-reaching ones. Many more parties are affected than we ever thought or permitted ourselves to imagine. "Me-firsters" don't care about the debris left in the wake of their actions, but mature, responsible adults do. They see not only the distinct ripples at the stone's entry point; they look for and anticipate the distant ones as well. In other words, they think as members of the moral community—as belonging to humanity.

Philosopher James Rachels has argued that if thinking as a member of the moral community isn't limited by place, neither is it limited by time.[4] Whether people will be affected by our actions now or years from now is irrelevant, for the stone we cast creates ripples of time as well as place. Our air and water are polluted, our food chain is contaminated, our solid waste mounts, our lush forests vanish. Our planet appears to be warming as its protective ozone layer thins. Looming, too: the dangers of nuclear waste disposal. How we deal with these threats will affect those who follow us as much as how former generations dealt with theirs affected us. We may reasonably debate exactly what we owe future generations, but we can't responsibly claim we owe them nothing, for, like us, they too will belong to humanity.[5]

Thinking as a member of the moral community, then, is comprehensive, global, and cross-generational thinking. It is not limited to the interests or concerns of any one group or people at any one place at any one time. It is indistinguishable from Albert Schweitzer's description of a "thinking being": "The man who has become a thinking being," said the physician-humanitarian, "feels a compulsion to give every will-to-live the same reverence for life that he gives his own."[6] But is this realistic? Is it too much, for example, to expect us to be concerned about life and lives distant in place or time?

Naturally, giving serious consideration to the interests of the world's hungry and the needs of future generations may seem remote from the exigencies of daily living. And it's true that such concerns probably do occupy the highest rungs on the ladder of beneficence. But what about several levels below? What about the very first rung, where we find incontestible duties never willfully to do harm? There is certainly nothing either remote or unrealistic about honoring this first priority of noninjury. Not deliberately injuring others is well within our reach, but often outside our grasp owing to a sadly deficient sense of the moral community.

Recall that businessman, for example, who created a jingling nuisance with his extravagant Christmas display. His sense of the moral community apparently was limited to his family; his neighborhood was literally his own front yard. True, he did protest that he would "walk through fire to help a stranger," but it took a court order to force him to respect the interests and rights of his neighbors, that is, to acknowledge *the* moral community as opposed to *his* moral community. In this case no one was being asked to feed a starving child an ocean away or plant a tree for future generations, but merely to exercise some self-control—to stop indulging himself at the expense of others.

Roughly the same could be said of the tax liars, insurance cheats, salad grazers, hotel thieves, highway litterers, reckless drivers, sexual predators, emotional manipulators, bill inflators, and apathetic bystanders, as well as overindulgent parents and their spoiled offspring, haughty diners and rude waitpersons, baiting students and short-tempered teachers, and all those who are too quick to sue and too slow to forgive. None of these individuals is being asked to do anything saintly or heroic, but the moral minimum: Do no harm.

———— • ◆ • ————

In the end, the borders of our moral community mark the borders of our moral world, and of our sense of personal responsibility. Becoming more self-responsible means taking the bird's-eye view of one's conduct—thinking about all the parties it might affect, not just those in any one place or at any one time. It means thinking of the impact of choices and actions in ever-widening ripples of concern. It means thinking like a good neighbor. "The good neighbor," said Martin Luther King Jr., "looks beyond the external accidents and discerns those inner qualities that make all men human and, therefore, brothers."[7] So *does the* responsible *neighbor.*

# 22. *Believing You Can Make a Difference, Then Doing What You Can*

The belief that you cannot make a difference stands like a roadblock on the path of self-responsibility. Just consider voter turnouts. Convinced that our single vote won't make any difference, we stay away from the ballot box in droves. No matter that many elections have turned on a mere handful of votes, and that increasingly a small minority of citizens is determining the political fate of the majority, including, of course, that self-declared insignificant nonvoter. Feeling that we don't really matter, we don't vote, nor feel any duty to.

Generally speaking, the more (or less) we believe we can change something, the more (or less) we feel obligated to. And what we believe we can't (or couldn't) affect, we'll ordinarily take no responsibility for. But even more important, the more we believe we can't make a difference, the greater the tendency to downplay and minimize our behavior. In other words, once persuaded that we don't matter, we tend to believe that little else does either, then behave accordingly. In this way actions get divorced from outcomes, especially harmful ones, which are dismissed as "no big deal." So the message is unmistakable: In order to become more responsible, we need to believe we can effect positive change. This empowering belief blunts a variety of responsibility dodges, from "Somebody should do something about that" and "I don't want to get involved" to "Don't sweat the small stuff" and "I was just following orders" to "I'm too old to change" and "But what else could I do? I was between a rock and a hard place." Thus, the millions of parents today who deplore drug use in theory but condone it in practice by treating drugs as an inevitable part of growing up. All the while these "buddy-parents" are clamoring for a war on drugs, they're weaseling out of their own private battles with dodges like "Oh well, I did it when I was that age and I turned out okay."

Like all foundational beliefs, the empowering belief that one matters takes shape (or not) early in life as part of the self-concept. Individuals who are raised to feel good about themselves—to see themselves as basically capable and adequate—generally grow to be self-confident adults. Those who are "toxically shamed"—therapist John Bradshaw's term for being made to feel essentially defective[1]—usually turn into self-doubting and self-loathing adults who more often believe they "can't" than they "can," as in: "I can't decide what to do," "I can't make up my mind," or "I can't make a difference." Underlying all the "I can'ts" is the corrosive belief "I don't matter."

Schools, of course, are another strong influence on one's self-confidence to effect positive change. Unfortunately, while perhaps too many of us teachers are confusing memorizing with understanding, too many of our students are asking: "But what does all this stuff have to do with 'real life'?" Not seeing—or being helped to see—any life-learning connection, they learn that what "really counts" is storing just enough information in short-term memory to get grades, get out, and get a job. In short, too many of our graduates have learned how to make a living, but not how to "live well." They know how to make money, but not how to make a difference. Mill said that "the worth of a State, in the long run, is the worth of the individuals composing it."[2] How much worth will a nation have that's composed of millions of individuals who have learned "what counts," but not that they count?

This is why it's heartening to see some colleges attempting to blend studies with community service. Today in institutions across the country can be found English majors who are producing newsletters for various service organizations; math students who are spending a night or two a week tutoring homeless children in math or reading; psychology majors who are volunteering at a group home for troubled teens; accounting majors who are helping the elderly prepare tax returns; and students across the curriculum tutoring inner-city schoolchildren and befriending AIDS patients.[3] These students are getting a lot more out of all this voluntarism than some course credit. They're heightening their social awareness, sharpening their desire to learn and improve so that they can help others, and enlarging their sense of self and of the moral community. By sharing the benefits and privilege of their education, they're enhancing its value to themselves. Most important, they're discovering that what they're learning in school makes a difference to someone—that they don't have to be rich to be generous, or famous to count. In caring for someone else, they're learning that someone else really does care about and depend on what they have to offer.

What's true of these students probably is true of most of us: Believing we can make a difference motivates us to do what we can. Thus, the cyclical relationship between the motivational principle "Believe you can make a difference" and the action principle "Do what you can." One drives the other. The more you believe you can make a difference, the more you'll do what you can, and, as a result, the more you'll believe you can make a difference.

Of course, simply because we can do something doesn't always mean we should. Many parents can well afford to give their child an expensive new car. Whether they should is another matter. Then, too, there are things we *can* do but generally shouldn't: lie, steal, cheat, or injure others, for example. But these and other notable exceptions aside, many things we can and even should do for ourselves and others, but don't. Why?

Sometimes we don't do what we can because we think we have to be "somebody" to make a difference. In a society as starstruck as ours, the ordinary person can feel puny and impotent. Constantly being invited to compare oneself to some carefully crafted image of power, success, or beauty, and endlessly exposed to the doings of the rich and famous, one easily can end up feeling deficient and inadequate, literally ashamed of oneself. What could so seriously flawed a creature possibly do that would amount to anything? Nothing—which is exactly what many of us do. "It is my duty, if I am a firefly," Henry Ward Beecher reminds those of such low self-regard, "to fly and sparkle, and fly and sparkle; not to shut my wings down over my phosphorescent self, because God did not make me a sun or a star."[4]

Other times we don't do what we can because we're too busy trying to do what we can't. Longfellow said that most people would succeed in small things if they weren't troubled with great ambitions. If we don't know and accept our limits, we can't set limits. We'll say yes when we should say no, and make promises we can't keep. We'll find ourselves chronically overextended and racing to keep up with commitments we had no business making. Our activity calendar will look more like the docket of a small claims court than of a reliable adult. Everything will be a priority, which means nothing comes first and first means nothing. Things will pile up, be neglected and mismanaged. Confusion will set in—activity will be mistaken for purpose, freneticism for meaning, and mediocrity for excellence. And while we're disappointing and perhaps harming others with our broken words and lame excuses, we'll probably blame them for the messes we've gotten ourselves into. We may even flatter ourselves that we're overloaded because, well, we're just too kind-hearted or overly zealous. In fact, we're irresponsible.

Besides feeling unimportant or not knowing our limits, casting situations in superhuman terms is still another big obstacle to doing what we can. Once we do that, we'll never see what we can possibly do to make a difference. Imagine, for example, if the aforementioned students had focused on world hunger rather than feeding some particular hungry person. Or suppose they had dwelled on eradicating disease rather than comforting some ill person. What if they had confined their thinking to wiping out illiteracy instead of teaching one individual to read and write? The sheer magnitude of the needs might have overwhelmed them. Feeling powerless, they might never have seen what they could do to make a difference. But instead of universalizing the need, they particularized it. By giving it a face and name, they could influence it. They saw what they could do, then did it.

In his *Hymns to an Unknown God,* philosopher Sam Keen reminds us that "it's not necessary to know our dreams for a just and compassionate world can come to pass in a short order. It's only necessary to follow a vocation that leads us in the right direction." Keen has no particular calling in mind. Any occupation or profession has the potential to summon us to what we can do, if we will merely listen to its call and respond—that is, be responsible. It says:

> You are an architect—shape space carefully to create bet-ter buildings and a more humane city for all citizens. You are a banker—work to create a more sustainable econ-omy. You are a farmer—tend the land so it will be fertile for generations to come. You are a physician—attend to the healing of the whole person. You are a cook—prepare meals that delight the palate and nourish the body. You are a CEO—create and market only those products that increase the common good. You are a soldier—minimize violence, keep the peace, and when you must fight, do so without hatred and the bitterness of revenge. You are a television producer—create stories that dignify, increase empathy, and inspire compassion.

"So long as we respond to the needs of the world by offer-ing our compassion and our skill," Keen writes, "we will not fall into despair at the overwhelming quantity of need."[5] We will live responsibly.

If a vocation has the potential to summon us to do what we can, why not other roles or activities? Thus:

- You are a parent—go in the direction you want your child to. As physician and educator Maria Montessori counseled: "Discipline for activity, for work, for good; not for immobility, not for passivity, not for obedience."[6]
- You are a student—unsettle your mind, train it in the use of its own powers. As Thomas Huxley suggested: "In matters of the intellect, follow your reason as far as it will take you." Escape the "blinding influence of traditional prejudice," and discern in the record of the past *"a reasonable ground of faith in [the] attainment of a noble future."*[7]
- You are a religionist—make an ally of tolerance, a foe of prejudice, and a companion of humility.
- You are a friend—be loyal, but never dishonest. Express and endure frank criticism. Be more concerned with meeting needs and honoring interests than winning approval. "Relieve the gloom of dark hours," as Ulysses S. Grant put it. Phone less, write more. Donne was right: Letters *do* mingle souls.[8] Be discreet.
- You are a life partner—listen. Communicate your needs and desires clearly, openly, honestly. Encourage the same of the other. Own your darker side, your weaknesses as well as your strengths. Value diversity. Respect complexity. Cherish nuance and surprise. Honor ritual. Be flexible and adaptable. Don't manipulate, cajole, or lecture. Understand more, judge less.
- You are a human being—love what you do, and do what you love. Remain curious. Don't turn your back on life. Heed Frost: Love what's loveable and hate what's hateable, and be wise enough to see the difference. Share your talent. Compromise, but never your-

self. Be somebody to someone. Learn from the wisdom, joys, and mistakes of others, and treat others as ends, never as means. Keep your word. Pay attention to the little things. Look for opportunity in setback, comfort in pain. Don't be unkind or proud. When you have nothing to say, say nothing. Live in the present. Lighten the burden of another—or at least don't add to it. Love others as you love yourself by holding both equally accountable to the highest standards of civility and morality.

———•◆•———

It is in the everyday circumstances of our lives that we discover how we can make a difference by doing what we can. We need look no further than to our homes, schools, neighborhoods, and workplaces—to our roles and activities—for occasions to practice responsible living. We need do no more than listen to their call and respond. If we do, then, to paraphrase Thoreau, we'll not merely be good, we'll be good for something.

# 23. *Forming Positive Associations and Having Exemplars*

For those who think that kids are pretty much the same today as they've always been, the February 14, 1996, edition of ABC's *Primetime Live* must have been sobering, drawing as it did a chilling profile of the values of thirty youngsters between the ages of eleven and sixteen. Whatever else might be said of these girls and boys—both black and white—let it not be said that they lacked candor. With a cynicism that belied their years, these middle-class kids batted back every question pitched, and then some:

- Would they lie, break a promise, or take a bribe? You bet, if something big were at stake, like money.
- What about following orders? Would they hurt, perhaps even kill, somebody if told to? Probably, so long as they didn't like the person and stood to profit.
- How about trying to save someone else's life, say a prisoner in a concentration camp? Nah, there's no advantage in risking your own hide for someone else.
- Was there anything they thought worth dying for? Hmm . . . money, maybe.

- What about adults they knew? Were most of them pretty decent? Not really. Most people would lie, break a promise, and do anything to get what they wanted.
- Surely they had some "heroes," individuals they really admired? The black children named several, the white children were stumped.

Understandably, this last revelation—that most of the kids couldn't name a single good person—really stunned their parents when they saw the taped interview. They couldn't understand their children's reactions, because they'd taught them to value truth, promises, and helping others. Perhaps they had. But maybe the problem wasn't *what* they were teaching but *how* they were teaching it. Maybe they needed to lecture less and model more—embody what they valued so that their kids could value what they embodied. But how to do this when possibly they themselves couldn't identify anyone they truly admired enough to be like and to urge their children to? Unfortunately, the interviewer never asked Mom and Dad to name someone they admired and drew their character strength from—"unfortunately" because none of us can be parents our children look up to unless we ourselves have figures we look up to. Basic to being an admirable person and parent is admiring others—having heroes.

In a recent speech at the Truman Library, author and former journalist Frank K. Kelly recounted his role in the 1948 marathon run Harry Truman made to retain the presidency. Although Truman's was a great personal victory, more than that, said Kelly, the man from Independence showed the nation that a person with fundamental virtues could overcome any odds. Kelly was referring to the thirty-third president's self-control and self-discipline; his courage and compassion; his loyalty and honesty; his faith and perseverance; and especially Truman's "keen sense of responsibility." "As I look back almost fifty years," said the author of *Memories of a True Man*, "I'm not sure that my participation in Truman's amazing drive in 1948 made any difference in the outcome, but I always felt a surge of joy when I remember that I worked for a man with so many virtues. . . . It changed my life."[1]

Frank Kelly's life-altering relationship will be familiar to those fortunate enough to have had a mentor show them the way, and perhaps envied by those not so fortunate. For better or worse, those we familiarly associate with have the strongest influence on us. They can move us in the direction of self-responsibility, as Truman did Kelly, or they can hurt us in that regard. Reason and duty enough, then, to choose carefully the company we keep.

But how do we know if the individuals we associate with are hurting or helping us be more responsible? What sorts of helping traits and behavioral patterns might we look for? Perhaps a good place to start is by insuring positive answers to the following questions:

- Are these individuals basically optimistic persons who believe in the possibility of change for the better, or are they basically pessimistic, negative, and cynical?
- Do they ordinarily view themselves as free and capable, or more as hapless victims of fate, circumstance, the system, or the wile of others?
- Do they rarely blame others?
- Do they keep their word and promises even when doing so is inconvenient?

- Do they show self-insight? admit that some of their beliefs could be incorrect and that they still may harbor prejudices, stereotypes, and assumptions they absorbed in growing up?
- Are they basically respectful of others, no matter how different they are from themselves? tolerant of views different from their own?
- Do they avoid viewing complex issues dichotomically—in either/or, black-and-white, right-and-wrong, "us vs. them" categories?
- Are they mainly "givers" rather than "takers"? generous with their time, talent, ideas, emotions?
- Does their idea of the moral community extend well beyond themselves, their families, and their groups?
- Do they honor themselves physically, emotionally, intellectually, and spiritually? Are they generally trying to move in the direction of growth and improvement in these areas?
- Are they free of emotion battering, spirit crushing, and life-destroying habits and addictions?
- Do they rate high in honesty, empathy, fairness, integrity, humility, courage, and responsibility?
- Do they ordinarily tell me when I'm wrong or just agree with me no matter what?
- Can I point to at least one specific, positive difference they have made in my life?
- Would I trust them with what I most cherish?

Although ordinarily not as influential as the company we keep, figures of fact and fiction can also be powerful models of responsible living or not. They can serve as exemplars—

examples of lives and qualities worth imitating—or not. From their courage and resolve, their compassion and empathy, their honesty and humility, their perseverance and principle, we can glean the full measure of responsible living. But this isn't easy in the culture of egotistical celebrity worship, which has descended so low that today being "clean"—not using drugs—or having babies *in* wedlock can qualify the "star" as a "role model." Rest assured we'll not find in arrested adolescents what we need to be responsible adults, but when the immature lack heroes, they'll make heroes of the immature.

For centuries for countless millions, the most prismatic exemplars, of course, have been the great religious figures: Jesus, Mohammed, Buddha (Sidhartha Gautama), Lao-tzu. But lustrous, too, is the life guided by "reasoned directed conscience," like Socrates'; or the one characterized by fidelity to noble purpose, like Martin Luther King Jr.'s; or the one iridescent with courage and conviction, like Rosa Parks's. (Happy to say, some of the black children in the *Primetime* discussion lab named King and Parks, but sadly, none of the white children did.) Then there are the young heroes, such as the selfless Harriet Tubman, who grew from a slave girl named "Minty" to a savior dubbed "Moses" for delivering her people to freedom via the Underground Railroad.[2] And Kate Shelley—another gritty young person, whose courage and determination sent her inching along the slippery track of a railroad bridge above a flood-swollen river in order to warn an oncoming train of the danger ahead.[3]

Fictive figures are no less inspiring than actual ones. What better symbol of honest labor, for example, than Longfellow's village blacksmith, who "earns whate'er he can?"[4] What more stirring a model of heroic self-sacrifice than Dickens's Sidney

Carton, who, comes the end of that fateful tale of two cities, pronounces his execution "a far, far better thing that I do, than I have ever done?"[5] And let's not forget the animals; they can get into the act, if we permit them. Why, it's from the mouth of that sagacious little fox in Antoine de Saint-Exupéry's *The Little Prince* that comes one of the most profound observations ever uttered about personal responsibility: "You become responsible, forever, for what you have tamed."[6] Which is to say: The ties we forge we must respect.

If our children lack exemplars, perhaps it's because we adults do. And if we do, little wonder. It's been duly noted elsewhere and often that we sadly live in a time of few public examples of what a mature and morally responsible individual is like. Just when we think we have chanced upon a woman or man of substance, the person is revealed to be a mountebank. What we took for high character turns out to be a carefully crafted mask. Behind the public image of a grown-up crouches an insecure little child who, at trouble's first sign, scurries behind the equivalent of Mama's apron: a phalanx of "spin doctors" and sophistic, alibiing mouthpieces. We feel the suffocating press of still another media-driven scandal in government, business, sports, entertainment, sometimes even in religion and academia. On our TV screens we glimpse the sordid lives of the rich and famous, which, while deserving our pity and contempt, are supposed to pique our curiosity and envy. Celebrity, it seems, is everything; anonymity alone is worse than death. There are, alas, few Harry Trumans these days.

For all that, there still remain rich veins of moral inspiration to be discovered and tapped for those willing to prospect more and spectate less. There is the shining example of Mother Teresa, that legendary symbol of love and compassion who has spent a lifetime helping the poor, the ill, the neglected, and the abandoned. And there is Aung San Suu Kyi, the Nobel Peace laureate who has been called a "symbol worldwide of democracy in chains." Likened to monumental figures like Nelson Mandela and Mahatma Gandhi, Suu Kyi always rejected government offers of freedom from imprisonment because they were conditioned on her leaving her country. What better proof that the history of liberty is the history of resistance?

But precisely because such individuals are truly extraordinary, their heroic lives and deeds can easily seem outside our reach. A hero, after all, is typically someone we look up to, not sideways at. And yet, others have expressed different, more attainable views, ones that ground heroism in the ordinary and commonplace. The French novelist Romain Rolland, for example, proclaimed a hero is "a man who does what he can. The others do not do it."[7] By this measure our lives are teeming with heroes, who, in doing what they can, offer compelling examples of highly responsible living. They demonstrate that it isn't only the trumpeted and singular who can teach basic truths and show new possibilities. The unsung and common can, too. But we need to fix our gaze on them, become better observers of our own backyards, where we will glimpse not only the wealthy philanthropists and community activists but many ordinary individuals doing exemplary things:

- the considerate next-door neighbors who show their children or grandchildren how to have fun without disrupting half the block

- the fellow worker who never gossips, complains, or drags personal problems into the workplace
- the parents of every color, income, and social class who would no more allow their young children to see a movie that they themselves hadn't previewed, no matter the rating, than they'd permit them to play with matches; parents who know that, like statistics, there are lies, damn lies, and ratings
- the brother who reads to his younger sister, and the father who encourages him to
- the affluent senior citizens who exhibit as much concern for the younger generations' welfare as they're inclined to give their own
- the baby "boomers" and "busters" who don't let the debt they've inherited blind them to the debt they owe past generations
- the able-bodied man who is too proud to take welfare and humble enough not to turn up his nose at honest work
- the doctors who practice gratis and the lawyers who work pro bono
- the young couples more concerned with how they will care for children than with having them

As we become more attuned to examples of mature adults in our neighborhoods and workplaces, we can also become more selective observers of what's occurring in other neighborhoods. Rather than allowing television, pulp magazines, and tabloid journalism to drag us down into the gutter of the latest juicy scandal or contrived controversy, we can use the media to help fill our minds with stories that uplift and are life-affirming. Granted they aren't given the coverage they deserve—virtue never sells like vice. But if we're interested in looking, we can find among the lurid and corrupt "daily news," reports here, references there, to individuals who are teaching by example, even if it isn't Christmas. Thus:

- the story of the train-ticket clerk who stays two hours after her shift ends, phoning social services to keep a runaway teenager from having to spend the night on the cold station floor; and her coworkers, who pool their money to buy a ticket home for a penniless woman
- the article about the newlyweds who change the flat of a young woman they chance upon one night weeping because her tire was blown out and she's stranded alone with no money for a tow
- the report of a clutch of police officers who spend their own time and money to burglarproof the home of a blind, eighty-year-old woman who has endured repeated break-ins;
- the tale of the bookstore browser who, still mindful of how she loved to read when she was the same age as the little girl who doesn't have enough money for the book she's selected, fishes into her purse and makes up the difference
- the account of a teenage, drug-addicted prostitute who secures a blanket from a drop-in center and drapes it over a stranger, another boy curled up, asleep and shivering
- the story of the fourteen-year-old girl who escorts a five-year-old three-quarters of a mile to a police sta-

tion when she finds the tyke leaning against a tree, crying because she's afraid to go home to a drunken father
- the item about the destitute family who turn in a wallet they find containing more than two thousand dollars in cash, a credit card, a passport, and a plane ticket.[8]

———•◆•———

Edmund Burke said that "Example is the school of mankind, and they will learn at no other."[9] If we want to be more responsible, we must surround ourselves with responsible people—fill our imaginations with them. And if we want our lives filled with responsible individuals, we ourselves must be more responsible. To have families and friends of principle, not expediency, we must own up and stand for something in our own right. For if learning is by example, we can only learn by seeing and teach by being.

# 24. *Living Wholeheartedly*

A man watched his brother die of an "unknown disease" he calls "half-heartedness." He writes:

> My brother's aging face reflected the closing of his heart. Once full of childhood wonder and surprise, it aged to a clown's mask covering dark cynicism. It looked like an engraved sneer. That mask became the way he dealt with the world, because he could no longer be deeply moved by the experiences of the heart.[1]

The writer, Jim Carolla, doesn't believe that his brother is that unusual. "We accept half-hearted life as a normal way to live," he says. "It has become so ingrained in our individual and collective psyche that we create institutions, professions, literature, and religions to support the sleep of the weak-hearted."[2]

*Weak-hearted* or *half-hearted* means exhibiting little interest or enthusiasm, as in a "halfhearted attempt to write a novel." *Wholehearted,* by contrast, is marked by unconditional commitment, unstinting devotion, unswerving enthusiasm, as in "wholehearted approval." Halfhearted is indecisive, tepid, irresolute. Wholehearted is sincere, earnest, candid.

It's also passionate, deep, intense, unfeigned, responsive, devout, and soulful.

Without wholeheartedness an individual is "a mere latent force and possibility," like a match awaiting the shock of a striking surface before it can spark.[3] He is, as Emerson said, always getting ready to live but never living—forever "on the edge of all that is great, yet . . . restrained in activity . . . always on the brink."[4] Ortega y Gasset, the Spanish philosopher, likened such individuals to "buoys that float on waves": They merely exist, avoiding difficulties and duties, making no effort to improve and perfect themselves.[5] The halfhearted feel quiet despair, but never sense the pulse of life within it. They spend their lives fleeing conflicts and issues that promise change and growth. Self-enfeebled by fear and uncertainty, they won't act; disillusioned and cynical, they see no reason to. They alibi and never realize that all alibis are stifling self-deceits. The halfhearted make excuses and never realize with Alexander Pope: "An excuse is worse and more terrible than a lie: For an excuse is a *lie guarded*."[6]

William Harvey, the seventeenth-century physician who discovered the circulation of blood in the human body, said that the heart is the "first principle of life" and the "sun of the microcosm." It is the heart, said Harvey, "by whose virtue and pulsation the blood is moved, perfected, quickened and preserved from corruption and lumpiness." To the famous anatomist the heart was "the household god [that] performs his office for the whole body by nourishing, cherishing and quickening, being the foundation of life and author of all things."[7]

If the heart is the beginning of our physical life, whole-heartedness is the beginning of our spiritual and moral life. It is the vital force that separates the living from the living dead. It heightens self-awareness, excites the imagination, sparks empathy, and sustains us in ever increasing and unfolding layers of consciousness. Wholeheartedness creates an insight environment by coaxing unconscious contents into consciousness, thereby awakening us to possibilities unglimpsed in the fog of cultural myths and symbolic imagery through which we must negotiate our lives. It quickens and nurtures our passion for life and our reverence for it. It protects us from the corruptions of faint-hearted living: fear, suspicion, anger, bitterness, cynicism, jealousy, insincerity, and apathy. If the heart is the foundation of our biological life, then *enormity* of heart is the foundation of our spiritual life—the passionate mainspring of all that is good, decent, and noble in us. It is the field of love, the source of all responsible action, the case that contains all those reasons that reason does not understand but needs to learn.

While some of us may be deaf to the language of the heart, others seem to know no other. Mitch Kinkannon, for example, was thirty-nine years old when he died in 1994 after living wholeheartedly with AIDS for five years. His death was part of the story he wanted told to help educate others. He succeeded with the distinguished assistance of reporter Rhonda Parks and photographer Mike Eliason, who were so captivated by this strong and gentle man that they thought his might make a "compelling subject for a story about AIDS." Thus began an odyssey covered frankly by the *Santa Barbara News-Press* in a series of articles spanning more than two years. At the end, AIDS had a face and name, and the people of the southern California resort community had a heroic example of how the responsible life is lived wholeheartedly.[8]

For most of the time, Parks remembers Kinkannon, a former member of a traveling circus, as happy and healthy, "a prankster with a . . . philosopher's way of looking at things." "I want to live as fully as possible," he once told her. "The dark side exists, but I don't have to dwell there."

But not despairing wasn't always easy. For one thing, there were the inevitable deaths of housemates at the AIDS home where he lived—thirty-four in all. Also inevitable: the phone calls that "dripped with venom and hatred" simply because he was a gay man with AIDS. But Kinkannon didn't let death or bigotry defeat him. He focused instead on the overwhelmingly positive reader response, to which he reacted with generosity and enthusiasm. Set on promoting better understanding of AIDS, he took his message to dozens of schools, colleges, and universities as well as to hospitals, support groups, and conferences across the nation, where he courageously shared his experience with thousands of people. He was determined, in short, to be the best example of someone living with AIDS, not dying of it.

At one national hospice conference, Kinkannon attributed his relative well-being to his appetite for life. "I'm not just a survivor," he told the audience of chaplains and nurses, psychotherapists and bioethicists, theologians and professors, hospice workers and grief counselors. "I'm a thriver." He cast his personal travail as "part of discovering the deeper meaning of humanity." "I am learning to love myself," he said, "and that means putting it into action and taking care of myself." He advised the sick and dying to "shift your perception if you can. Don't buy into the thought that it has to be suffering and terrible. Sure, there is some of that, but it doesn't mean you have to let it rule your life."

To the many who were comforted by his words and moved by his sharing to deepen their sense of neighborly love, Kinkannon responded with equal parts humility and gratitude. "To share what I have is an opportunity of a lifetime," he told them. "I am an ordinary human being. But we're all extraordinary in some way. Some people just don't know it yet. . . . Sometimes we touch someone's heart without ever knowing it. If I can reach just one person, I feel I have honored myself. I am a good person."

A few hours before his death, Parks reports that Mitch thanked the many people who read the articles about him. "I know I touched them and made a difference," he said. "I'll die in peace knowing I made my mark on the world."

It was Coleridge who said that what comes from the heart goes to the heart. Much came from Mitch Kinkannon's heart: honesty, enthusiasm, zest for life, sense of purpose, love, and care. But beyond this, what also must go to the heart of everyone who came to know him, because it came so forcefully from his own, is that wholehearted living is always having hope. It is avoiding the great evil of premature departure. It is always believing in "the possibility of choice," Archibald MacLeish's phrase for creating alternatives for one's self. Without the possibility of choice and its exercise, we're not human beings but things, instruments.

If it's the "possibility of choice" that stamps our humanity, then it's the ability to accept responsibility that takes our measure. When the only freedom we wish for is the freedom *from* responsibility, then, like nations, we cease to be free. When we forsake the possibility of choice for the comfort of security, we slip into the sleep of the weak-hearted.

————— • ◆ • —————

"The tragedy of life is not in the fact of death," said Norman Cousins, "but in what dies inside [us] while [we] live."[9] When we can "no longer be deeply moved by the experiences of the heart," the heart ceases to be deeply moved by life. Wonder dies, and with it interest, then caring, and, ultimately, soul. And then, when we become like "human owls"—"vigilant in darkness, and blind to light, mousing for vermin, and never seeing noble game"[10]—we find nothing worth the effort, not even ourselves. But it needn't be that way, as the Kinkannons aplenty continue to prove. For so long as we keep alive what's best in us—so long as we can "warm both hands by the fire of life"[11]—our capacity to respond to the world lives, and so, too, our sense of responsibility for it—and the hope that keeps the heart from breaking.

# Notes

## Part I  *Avoiding Personal Responsibility*

### Introduction:  Language of Excuse and Evasion

1. William J. Bennett, *The Book of Virtues* (New York: Simon & Schuster, 1993), p. 185.
2. George Orwell, "Politics and the English Language," in *Shooting an Elephant* (New York: Harcourt, Brace & World, 1950), p. 92.
3. Walt Whitman, "Slang in America," *The Works of Walt Whitman* (New York: Funk & Wagnalls, 1968), vol. 2, p. 421.
4. Leonard Bernstein and Stephen Sondheim, *West Side Story*, vocal score (New York: G. Schirmer, Inc., and Chappell & Co., Inc., 1959), pp. 165–78.
5. "Why Woman Told Story About Gingrich," *San Francisco Chronicle*, 19 August 1995, p. A6.

### Chapter 1.  "Here's Another Fine Mess You've Gotten Me Into"

1. Tom Gorman, "Jury Awards Robber an Additional $80,000," *Los Angeles Times*, 27 April 1995, p. A3.
2. Ann Landers, "Lots of Pain and Suffering," *The Sunday Oregonian*, 4 June 1994, p. L4.

## Chapter 2. "Don't Blame Me,
## I Didn't Vote for Him/Her"

1.  Henry Adams, *The Education of Henry Adams* (New York: The Modern Library, 1931), p. 7.
2.  H. L. Mencken, *Minority Report: H. L. Mencken's Notebooks* (New York: Knopf, 1956), p. 222.
3.  Michel de Montaigne, "Of Presumption," in *The Complete Essays of Montaigne*, trans. Donald L. Frame (Stanford, CA. Stanford University Press, 1943), Book 2, p. 498.
4.  Theodore Roosevelt, "The Roosevelt Doctrine," delivered to the New York Chamber of Commerce, November 11, 1902.

## Chapter 3. "I Didn't Want to Get Involved"

1.  James Coates, "Rescuers Braved Mob's Savagery to Save Driver," *Santa Barbara News-Press*, 3 May 1992, p. B10.
2.  Ibid.
3.  Ibid.
4.  James Rachels, "What Would a Satisfactory Moral Theory Be Like?" *The Elements of Moral Philosophy* (New York: Random House, 1986), p. 144.
5.  William Frankena, *Ethics* (Englewood Cliffs, NJ: Prentice-Hall, 1973), p. 69.
6.  Ibid., p. 70.
7.  David Hume, *An Enquiry Concerning the Principles of Morals* (Chicago: The Open Court Publishing Co., 1912), p. 109.
8.  Rollo May, *The Courage to Create* (New York: Bantam Books, 1976), pp. 8–9.

## Chapter 4. "How Was I Supposed to Know?"

1.  Ambrose Bierce, *The Enlarged Devil's Dictionary*, ed. Ernest Jerome Hopkins (Garden City, NY: Doubleday & Company, 1967), p. 14.
2.  Mei-Ling Hopgood and Alison Young, "Talk Show Guest Held in Slaying of His 'Secret Admirer'," *Santa Barbara News-Press*, 10 March 1995, p. A3.

3.  Howard Rosenberg, "When a Talk Show's Surprise Backfires," *Los Angeles Times*, 13 March 1995, p. F1.
4.  Ron French, " 'Jenny Jones' Case Changing the Tone of TV Talk Shows," *USA Today*, 28 February 1996, p. 6A.
5.  "He receives comfort like cold porridge." William Shakespeare, *The Tempest*, Act 2, Scene 1, Line 10.

**Chapter 5. "It's Not in My Job Description"**
1.  Michael Davis, "Explaining Wrongdoing," *Journal of Social Philosophy* 20 (Spring/Fall, 1989) p. 80.

**Chapter 6. "The Computer Is Down"**
1.  Henry Ward Beecher, *Proverbs from Plymouth Pulpit*, ed. William Drysdale (New York: D. Appleton and Company, 1887), p. 44.
2.  Henry David Thoreau, *Walden* (New York: Branball House, 1951), p. 51.
3.  Erich Fromm, *The Sane Society* (New York: Rinehart & Company, 1955), p. 360.
4.  For the "social interface" trend, see: Amy Harmon, "Putting Personality Into Your PC," *Los Angeles Times*, 13 January 1995, p. A1.
5.  For the mad rush to buy computers and get on-line, see: Leslie Helm, "Getting Lost in Cyberspace," *Los Angeles Times*, 16 December 1994, p. A1.
6.  Rheingold as quoted in Bob Sipchen, "The Techno Traitor," *Los Angeles Times*, 27 March 1995, p. E1.
7.  For the profile of the world of "players," see: Douglas Birch, "Just a Little Too Tangled Up in the Internet," *Los Angeles Times*, 5 September 1994, p. E1. For impact of high-tech electronics on kids, see: Mary Pipher, *The Shelter of Each Other* (New York: Putnam, 1996).
8.  Jeff Leeds, "Runaway in E-Mail Case Is Reunited With Her Parents," *Los Angeles Times*, 13 June 1995, p. E1.

**Chapter 7. "But I Thought You Were on the Pill!"**
1.  Dr. Laura Schlessinger, *How Could You Do That?!* (New York: HarperCollins, 1996), p. 80.

2. Ibid.

3. "God made Adam master over all creatures, to rule over all living things, but when Eve persuaded him that he was lord even over God she spoiled everything. We have you women to thank for that! With tricks and cunning women deceive men, as I, too, have experienced." Martin Luther, "Table Talk," *Luther's Works*, trans. and ed. Theodore G. Tappert (Philadelphia: Fortress Press, 1967), Vol. 54, pp. 174–75.

4. James Boswell, *The Life of Samuel Johnson*, LL.D. (New York: The Heritage Press, 1963), Vol. 1, p. 328.

5. Arthur Schopenhauer, "Studies in Pessimism," *Complete Essays of Schopenhauer*, trans. T. Bailey Saunders (New York: Wiley Book Company, 1942), Book V, pp. 79–80.

6. Thomas Huxley, "Emancipation—Black and White," *Lay Sermons, Addresses, and Reviews* (London: MacMillan and Co., 1880), p. 24.

7. Schlessinger, p. 81.

8. Sir Walter Scott, *Marmion*, in *The Complete Works of Sir Walter Scott*, ed. Horace E. Scudder (Boston: Houghton Mifflin, 1900), Canto 6, Stanza 17.

9. Eric Hoffer, *The Passionate State of Mind* (New York: Harper & Row, Publishers, 1955), p. 76.

**Chapter 8. "As a (Whatever), I Got a Right"**

1. Donella H. Meadows, "Pay Me to Be Good—or I'll Sue," *Los Angeles Times*, 10 March 1995, p. B7.

2. Reinhold Niebuhr, *Moral Man and Immoral Society* (New York: Charles Scribner's Sons, 1953), pp. xi–xii.

3. Ibid., p. 273.

**Chapter 9. "It's Legal, Isn't It?"**

1. William Shaw and Vincent Barry, *Moral Issues in Business*, 6th ed. (Belmont, CA: Wadsworth, 1995), p. 28.

2. H. L. Mencken, *A Mencken Chrestomathy* (New York: Vintage Books, 1982), p. 623.

3. Edmund Burke, *Burke's Letters on a Regicide Peace* (London: George Bell & Sons, 1893), p. 66.

4. Henry David Thoreau, "Essay on Civil Disobedience," in *The Portable Thoreau*, ed. Carle Bode (New York: Viking Press, 1947), p. 111.

## Chapter 10. "Don't Sweat the Small Stuff"
1. Craig Thomashoff, "America's Least Wanted Criminals," *Los Angeles Times*, 10 May 1993, p. E6.
2. Frances M. Barbour, *A Concordance to the Sayings in Franklin's Poor Richard* (Detroit: Gale Research Company, 1974), p. 146.
3. Epictetus, "Of Steadfastness," *Discourses*, in *Epictetus: The Discourses, The Manual, and Fragments*, trans. W. A. Oldfather (Cambridge, MA: Harvard University Press, 1979), Vol. 1, pp. 191–92.

## Chapter 11. "Look Out for Number 1"
1. Michael Arkush, "The Pastry Maker's Life Is a Recipe for Pursuit of Perfection," *Los Angeles Times*, 4 March 1995, p. B1.
2. Robert C. Solomon and Kristine Hanson, "Why Ethics?" in *It's Good Business* (New York: Atheneum, 1985), p. 12.
3. Ibid.
4. Henri Amiel, *Amiel's Journal*, trans. Mrs. Humphrey Ward (New York: Macmillan Company, 1904), entry dated December 16, 1856, p. 61.
5. Alfred Adler, *What Life Should Mean to You* (New York: Blue Ribbon Books, 1931), p. 197.
6. Martin Luther King Jr., "Racism and the White Backlash," in *Where Do We Go From Here: Community or Chaos?* (Boston: Beacon Press, 1968), p. 72.
7. Ibid., p. 73.
8. Richard Paul, *Critical Thinking Handbook* (Rohnert Park, CA: Center for Critical Thinking and Moral Critique, 1987).
9. Michel de Montaigne, "Of Experience," in *The Complete Essays of Montaigne*, trans. Donald L. Frame (Stanford, CA: Stanford University Press, 1943), Book 3, p. 825.

### Chapter 12. "Charity Begins at Home"

1.  John Keats, "Letter to George and Thomas Keats," dated 13 January 1818, *Complete Poems and Selected Letters* (New York: The Odyssey Press, 1935), p. 529.

2.  Dennis Cauchon, "Court Pulls Plug on Little Rock Lights," *USA Today*, 6 December 1994, p. 1A.

3.  Ibid.

4.  *The Collects from The Book of Common Prayer* (Chiswick Bedford Park: Caradoc Press, 1901), Quinquagesima Sunday.

5.  For the study and in-depth interviews supporting both these statistics and a three-year project on religious and economic values and beliefs, see: Robert Wuthnow, *Sharing the Journey* (New York: Free Press, 1994).

6.  Charles Dickens, *Martin Chuzzlewit* (New York: Alfred A. Knopf, 1947), p. 400.

### Chapter 13. "I Was Just Following Orders"

1.  Christopher R. Browning, *Ordinary Men: Reserve Police Battalion 101 and the Final Solution in Poland* (New York: HarperCollins Publishers, 1992). For an indictment of "ordinary Germans," see: Daniel Jonah Goldhagen, *Hitler's Willing Executioners* (New York: Knopf, 1996).

2.  John Stuart Mill, "On Liberty," *Essential Works of John Stuart Mill*, ed. Max Lerner (New York: Bantam Books, 1961), Part 3, p. 310.

3.  Browning, pp. 8–9.

4.  Gordon Allport, *The Nature of Prejudice* (Cambridge, MA: Addison-Wesley Publishing Company, 1954), p. 29.

5.  Hitler, cold warriors, and "electronic church" examples cited in Anthony Pratkanis and Elliot Aronson, *Age of Propaganda* (New York: W. H. Freeman and Company, 1991), p. 172.

6.  Ibid.

7.  Konrad Lorenz, *On Aggression*, trans. Marjorie Kerr Wilson (New York: Harcourt, Brace & World, 1963), p. 274.

## Chapter 14. "But What Else Could I Do?
## I Was Between a Rock and a Hard Place"

1. Blaise Pascal, *Pensées: Thoughts on Religion and Other Subjects*, trans. William Finlayson Trotter, eds. H. S. Thayer and Elizabeth B. Thayer (New York: Washington Square Press, 1965), #100, pp. 34–35.
2. "Maybe all we can do is hope to end up with the right regrets." Arthur Miller, *The Ride Down Mount Morgan* (New York: Penguin Books, 1991), Act 1.

## Chapter 15. "The Devil Made Me Do It"

1. William Shakespeare, *King Lear*, Act I, Scene 2, Line 112.
2. G. E. Zuriff, "Medicalizing Character," *Public Interest*, Spring 1996, pp. 94–99.
3. Don Van Natta Jr., "Judge Assaulted Over Drug Case Issues Reversal and an Apology," *The New York Times*, 2 April 1996, p. A1.
4. Ann Landers, "Sexual Drive Needs Directions to Home," *Los Angeles Times*, 3 March 1995, p. E2.
5. Richard L. Berke, "For Voters, Hope Gives Way to Anger, Fear and Cynicism," *The New York Times*, 10 October 1994, p. A1.
6. Garrison Keillor, "A Nation of Soreheads," *The New York Times*, 23 October 1994, p. E15.
7. Russell Baker, "And He Is Us," *The New York Times*, 26 November 1994, p. 23.

## Chapter 16. "Boys Will Be Boys"

1. For shopworn stereotypes, see: Robin Abcarian, "Spur Posse Case—The Same Old (Sad) Story," *Los Angeles Times*, 17 April 1993, p. E1.
2. Statistics cited in Judith Sherven and James Sniechowski, "Why Women Stay with Abusers," *USA Today*, 24 January 1995, p. 11A.
3. Ibid.
4. Ibid.

5.   Epictetus, "The Average Person and the Philosopher," *A Dialogue in Common Sense*, trans. John Bonforte (New York: Philosophical Library, 1974), p. 128.

### Chapter 17. "I'm Too Old to Change"
1.   Juvenal, "Satire 11," *The Satires,* trans. Niall Rudd (Oxford: Clarendon Press, 1991), p. 100.
2.   William Shakespeare, "The Passionate Pilgrim," *The Poems* (Cambridge, England: University Press, 1966), p. 116.
3.   Benjamin Disraeli, *Coningsby* (New York: E.P. Dutton & Co., 1911), p. 98.
4.   T. S. Eliot, "Gerontion," *The Complete Poems and Plays 1909–1950* (New York: Harcourt, Brace & World, 1971), p. 21.
5.   Henri Amiel, *Amiel's Journal*, trans. Mrs. Humphrey Ward (New York: Macmillan Company, 1904), entry dated September 21, 1874, p. 218.
6.   W. H. Auden, *The Age of Anxiety: A Baroque Eclogue* (New York: Random House, 1947), p. 134.
7.   Lucius Annaeus Seneca, "On Tranquillity of Mind," *Moral Essays*, trans. John W. Basore (Cambridge, MA: Harvard University Press, 1958), Vol. 2, p. 233.
8.   "Unregarded age in corners thrown." Shakespeare, *As You Like It,* Act 2, Scene 3, Line 42.
9.   Simone de Beauvoir, *The Coming of Age,* trans. Patrick O'Brian (New York: G. P. Putnam's Sons, 1972), pp. 540–41.
10.  "to change . . . endlessly." Henri Bergson, *Creative Evolution* (New York: The Modern Library, 1944), p. 10.

## Part II  *Embracing Personal Responsibility*
### Introduction:  Mainsprings of Responsibility
1.   Plato, "Crito," *Plato: The Last Days of Socrates,* trans. Hugh Tredennick (New York: Penguin Books, 1969), p. 87.
2.   William Bennett, *The Book of Virtues* (New York: Simon and Schuster, 1993) p. 246.
3.   George Orwell, "Politics and the English Language," in *Shooting an Elephant* (New York: Harcourt, Brace & World 1950), p. 77.

4.  *Bill Moyers: World of Ideas II*, ed. Andie Tucher (New York: Doubleday, 1990), p. 162.
5.  William Wordsworth, "The Tables Turned," *William Wordsworth Complete Poetical Works*, ed. Bliss Perry (Boston: Houghton Mifflin and Company, 1904), line 21, p. 83.

## Chapter 18.  Recasting Your Fear
1.  Ralph Waldo Emerson, *Nature, Addresses, and Lectures* (Cambridge, MA: Riverside Press, 1876), p. 104.
2.  Pierre Teilhard de Chardin, *The Phenomenon of Man* (New York: Harper Brothers Publishers, 1959), p. 265.
3.  Thornton Wilder, *The Bridge of San Luis Rey* (New York: Longmans, Green and Co., 1935), p. 140.
4.  George Bernard Shaw, *Candida*, in *Complete Plays with Prefaces* (New York: Dodd, Mead and Company, 1962), Vol. 3, p. 204.

## Chapter 19.  Knowing Yourself
1.  Blaise Pascal, *Pensées; Thoughts on Religion and Other Subjects*, trans. William Finlayson Trotter, eds. H. S. Thayer and Elizabeth B. Thayer (New York: Washington Square Press, 1965) #66, p. 18.
2.  Alfred, Lord Tennyson, "Oenone," in *Poetical Works of Alfred, Lord Tennyson* (London: Macmillan and Co., 1899), lines 142–43, p. 42.
3.  James Baldwin, *Nobody Knows My Name* (New York: Dell Publishing Co., 1961), p. xi.
4.  Marcus Tullius Cicero, *De Legibus (Laws)*, trans. Clinton Walker Keyes (Cambridge, MA: Harvard University Press, 1977), p. 365.
5.  Vincent Ryan Ruggiero, *Beyond Feelings: A Guide to Critical Thinking*, 3rd ed. (Mountain View, CA: Mayfield Publishing Co., 1990), pp. 121–22.
6.  Tom Cunningham, *King Baby* (Center City, MN: Hazelden, 1986).
7.  Ben Jonson, "To the Memory of William Shakespeare," in *Complete Poetry of Ben Jonson*, ed., William B. Hunter Jr.

(Garden City, NY: Doubleday & Company, 1963), line 43, p. 373.

8. Hermann Hesse, *Demian*, trans. Michael Roloff and Michael Lebeck (New York: Harper & Row, Publishers, 1965), p. 46.

9. George Bernard Shaw, *Maxims In Revolutionists* in *Complete Plays with Prefaces* (New York: Dodd, Mead and Company, 1962), Vol. 3, p. 732.

10. Plato, "Apology," *Dialogues of Plato*, ed. Justin D. Kaplan (New York: Pocket Books, 1950), p. 34.

11. Thomas S. Szasz, *Law, Liberty and Psychiatry: An Enquiry into the Social Uses of Mental Health Practices* (New York: The Macmillan Company, 1963), p. 255.

## Chapter 20. Letting Your Conscience Be Your Guide, Not Your God

1. William Shakespeare, *Henry the Eighth*, Act 3, Scene 2, Line 379.

2. Albert Schweitzer, *The Philosophy of Civilization*, trans. C.T. Campion (Tallahassee: University Presses of Florida, 1981), p. 318.

3. Edward Young, *Night Thoughts*, ed. Steven Cornford (Cambridge: Cambridge University Press, 1989), p. 53.

4. It was Thomas Hobbes who noted the potential of the conscience, like judgment, for error: "Another doctrine repugnant to civil society is that *whatsoever a man does against his conscience is sin;* and it dependeth on the presumption of making himself judge of good and evil. For a man's conscience and his judgement is the same thing, and as the judgement, so also the conscience, may be erroneous." Thomas Hobbes *Leviathan*, ed. Michael Oakshot (Oxford: Basil Blackwell, 1946), pt. 2, ch. 29, p. 211.

5. Credit goes to Bill Shaw for the Huck Finn example, William Shaw and Vincent Barry, *Moral Issues in Business*, 6th ed. (Belmont, CA: Wordsworth, 1995), p. 14.

6. Mark Twain, *The Adventures of Huckleberry Finn* (New York: Harper & Brothers Publishers, Inc., 1912), pp. 125–26.

7. Michel de Montaigne, "Of Custom," in *The Complete Essays of Montaigne*, trans. Donald L. Frame (Stanford, CA: Stanford University Press, 1943), p. 83.
8. Ibid.

## Chapter 21. Thinking As a Member of the Moral Community

1. Alfred Adler, *Social Interest: A Challenge to Mankind*, trans. John Linton and Richard Vaughn (London: Faber and Faber, 1938), p. 38.
2. William Hazlitt, "American Literature—Dr. Channing," *Complete Works of William Hazlitt*, ed. P. P. Howe (London: J. M. Dent & Sons, 1933), Vol. 16, p. 332.
3. *The American Heritage Dictionary of the English Language*, 3rd edition (Boston: Houghton Mifflin Company, 1992), p. 1210.
4. James Rachels, "What Would a Satisfactory Moral Theory Be Like?" in *The Elements of Moral Philosophy* (New York: Reading House, 1986), p. 145.
5. For obligations to future generations, see: Joel Feinberg, "The Rights of Animals and Unborn Generations," in *Philosophy and Environmental Crisis*, ed. William T. Blackstone (Athens, GA: University of Georgia Press, 1974), pp. 43–68.
6. Schweitzer, *The Philisophy of Civilization*, trans, C. T. Campion (Tallahassee: University Presses of Florida, 1981), p. 309.
7. Martin Luther King, Jr., *Strength to Love* (New York: Harper & Row Publishers, 1963), p. 19.

## Chapter 22. Believing You Can Make a Difference, Then Doing What You Can

1. John Bradshaw, *Healing the Shame That Binds You* (Deerfield Park, FLa.: Health Communications, 1988), p. 5.
2. John Stuart Mill, "On Liberty," in *Essential Works of John Stuart Mill*, ed. Max Lerner (New York: Bantam Books, 1961), part 5, p. 360.
3. Jennifer Warren, "Venturing Beyond Ivy Walls," *Los Angeles Times*, 23 May 1993, p. 1.

4. Henry Ward Beecher, *Life Thoughts* (Boston: Phillips, Sampson and Company, 1858), p. 285.
5. Sam Keen, *Hymns to an Unknown God: Awakening the Spirit in Everyday Life* (New York: Bantam Books, 1994), p. 245.
6. Maria Montessori, *The Montessori Method*, trans. Anne E. George (New York: Frederick A. Stokes Company, 1912), p. 93.
7. Thomas Huxley quoted in *What Great Men Think of Religion*, ed. Ira Cardiff (New York: Arno Press & *The New York Times*, 1972), pp. 188–190.
8. John Donne, *The Complete Poetry and Selected Prose of John Donne*, ed. Charles M. Coffin (New York: The Modern Library, 1952), p. 129.

## Chapter 23. Forming Positive Associations and Having Exemplars

1. Frank K. Kelly, "Harry Truman—Real Memories of a True Man," *Santa Barbara News-Press*, 9 April 1995, p. G2.
2. For a recent Tubman biography, see: Ann Petry, *Harriet Tubman: Conductor in the Underground Railroad* (New York: Harper Trophy, 1995).
3. For the Shelley story, see: Robert San Souci, *Kate Shelley Bound for Legend* (New York: Dial Books for Young Readers, 1995).
4. "He earns whate'er he can, / And looks the whole world in the face, / For he owes not any man." Henry Wadsworth Longfellow, "The Village Blacksmith," *The Works of Henry Wadsworth Longfellow* (New York: The DAVOS Press, 1909), vol. 4, p. 215.
5. Charles Dickens, *A Tale of Two Cities* (New York: Thomas Y. Cromwell & Company, 1904), p. 400.
6. Antoine de Saint-Exupéry, *The Little Prince*, trans. Katherine Woods (New York: Harcourt, Brace & World, 1941), p. 71.
7. Romain Rolland, *Jean-Christophe*, trans. Gilbert Cannan (New York: Henry Holt and Company, 1913), Book 1, p. 353.

8.  Catherine Gewertz, "Underneath LA's Tough Skin Beats a Heart of Gold," *Los Angeles Times*, 27 November 1994, p. E8.

9.  Edmund Burke, *Burke's Letters on a Regicide Peace* (London George Bell & Sons, 1893), p. 84.

## Chapter 24. Living Wholeheartedly

1.  Jim Carolla, "The Magic of Childhood Grows Hard in Adults," *Los Angeles Times*, November 21, 1994, p. E3.

2.  Ibid.

3.  Henri Amiel, *Amiel's Journal*, trans. Mrs. Humphrey Ward (New York: Macmillan Company, 1904), entry dated December 17, 1856, p. 61.

4.  Ralph Waldo Emerson, *Journals of Waldo Emerson*, eds. Edward Waldo Emerson and Waldo Emerson Forbes (Boston: Houghton Mifflin Company, 1910), Vol. 3, Journal xxv, p. 239.

5.  José Ortega y Gasset, *The Revolt of the Masses* (New York: W. W. Norton & Company, Inc., 1932), p. 15.

6.  Alexander Pope, *The Prose of Alexander Pope*, ed. Rosemary Cowler (Hamden, CT: Archon Books, 1986), Vol. 2, p. 161.

7.  William Harvey, *The Movement of the Heart and Blood*, trans. Gweneth Whitteridge (London: Blackwell Scientific Publications, 1976), p. 76.

8.  The facts of the Kinkannon case, including quotations, are drawn mainly from the following articles that appeared in the *Santa Barbara News-Press*. In all instances, Rhonda Parks is the reporter and Mike Eliason the photographer: "Mitch's Story," 14 July 1993, p. B6; "Illness Deals Heavy Blow," 28 November 1993, p. A10; "Mitch's Story Comes to Quiet, Loving End," 9 February 1994, p. A1; "Recalling a Life Full of Passion, Will to Survive," 13 February 1994, p. A1; "Those He Touched Honor Kinkannon," 13 February 1994, A1; "Friends to Carry Legacy of Kinkannon's Efforts," 13 February 1994, p. A8.

9.  Norman Cousins, *The Celebration of Life: A Dialogue on Immortality and Infinity* (New York: Harper & Row, 1974), p. 71.

10.  Henry Ward Beecher, *Proverbs from Plymouth Pulpit*, William Drysdale (New York: D. Appleton and Company, 1887) p. 49.

11.  The line is from Walter Savage Landor's "Dying Speech of an Old Philosopher," in *Poems by Walter Savage Landor*, ed. Geoffrey Grigson (Carbondale, IL: Southern Illinois Press, 1965), p. 172.

# About the Author

In 1969, shortly after returning from a two-year stint as a teacher with the Peace Corps in Uganda, East Africa, Vincent Barry began a career in higher education that continues today. He is a professor at Bakersfield College in Southern California, where he has taught a variety of courses over the past 28 years, including two in applied ethics: Business and Social Responsibility, and Ethics for Living and Dying.

His first serious writing efforts were two one-act plays, both produced off-Broadway in 1972 at the American Place Theatre. A year later he had several plays selected for representation by the University of Minnesota's Office for Advanced Drama Research, a program in experimental theatre. During the past twenty years he has authored and coauthored numerous college textbooks in the fields of introductory philosophy, logic, critical thinking, general ethics, and business ethics. His texts have been used in hundreds of colleges and universities by thousands of students. He currently lives in Santa Barbara, California, with his wife.